PETER
CROUCH
SUPER STRIKER

PETER
CROUCH
SUPER STRIKER

IAN CRUISE

JOHN BLAKE

Published by John Blake Publishing Ltd,
3 Bramber Court, 2 Bramber Road,
London W14 9PB, England

www.blake.co.uk

First published in hardback in 2007

ISBN: 978 1 84454 374 8

British Library Cataloguing-in-Publication Data:

A catalogue record for this book is available from the British Library.

Design by www.envydesign.co.uk

Printed in Great Britain by CPD, Wales

1 3 5 7 9 10 8 6 4 2

Papers used by John Blake Publishing are natural, recyclable products made
from wood grown in sustainable forests. The manufacturing processes conform
to the environmental regulations of the country of origin.

All pictures reproduced by kind permission of Offside, with the exception of the
pictures on Page 3, above and below left; page 5 which are reproduced by kind
permission of Cleva.

CONTENTS

PREFACE

It's debatable whether any player in English football history has polarised opinion in quite the same way as Peter Crouch has done.

Pub debates have raged far and wide in the past couple of years as people have queued up to knock him or praise him, depending on their own particular point of view.

The fans on the streets are divided, and so too are the experts. For every TV pundit in the pro-Crouch corner, you are likely to find a fully paid-up member of the anti-Crouch brigade. It's a debate that seems set to run and run, no matter what he does on the pitch.

Every time he scores a spectacular goal – and there have been several – he is lauded as having 'good feet for a big man' and praised for his technique. Every time he misses a presentable opportunity, he is derided as some sort of circus sideshow who has no place on a football pitch.

Indeed, Arsene Wenger once referred to him as a

'basketball player' after his Arsenal side had played Southampton. And when Wenger – a man who has proved time and time again at the north London club that he has an eye for spotting a talented player – says something like that, well, people are bound to listen and their opinions are bound to be swayed.

Crouch, though, took the attack in his stride. He said at the time, 'If people are having a dig at me, I have to take it as a compliment. I had just scored the equaliser against Wenger's team and he was probably angry. I'm pleased about that. If I was anonymous, he wouldn't have mentioned me.'

Former Arsenal and Republic of Ireland striker Niall Quinn, a player Crouch has been likened to because of their similar statures, also slated Crouch's technical ability and reading of the game in a newspaper column, claiming he was naive in some of his off-the-ball movement.

Crouch's response? 'I read that,' he said. 'Quinn talked a lot of sense and it opened my eyes. He was a similar player to me – and a great player – and it's always helpful to hear things from people who have been there and done it. He was talking about making more angled runs, how to lead the line and how to get on the end of things. It was a good article.'

And, even when he was being jeered and abused by his own fans as he prepared to come on for England against Poland at Old Trafford in October 2005, he refused to be downhearted.

Instead, he claimed, 'I heard it, it was not nice, but I was a Liverpool player coming on at Old Trafford. I honestly didn't think too much about it. If I had, I'd probably have crumbled. I manage to block a lot of that stuff out. It's my way of dealing with things and it has stood me in good stead so far.'

Whatever has been written or said about him, no one can argue about his temperament and his determination to get the absolute maximum out of the talent he has been blessed with ... or cursed with, depending on which way you look at it.

Crouch has never let the doubters and the cynics – of whom there have been many – distract him from his long-term goal of proving himself as one of the leading strikers in the country. Even when he endured a dreadful barren run during the early months of his Liverpool career, he refused to let his head drop and continued to battle until things came right. Now, he can do no wrong in the eyes of the Reds fans who sing his praises from the Kop.

'He's big, he's red, his feet stick out the bed ... Peter Crouch ... Peter Crouch...' they chant from the stands at Anfield, and he is now a confirmed favourite of the Liverpool supporters.

A blog on a Liverpool website said, 'Peter Crouch does not pass water. He takes it on his chest, holds it up, then passes water. Traffic delays don't just happen – they happen because Peter Crouch is there and Crouch can hold up anything.'

But it has certainly not been plain sailing for the man himself to get to the top; he has had to live with taunts of 'freak' and 'beanpole' from an early age. Quite simply, when you're 6ft 7in, there aren't too many places to hide.

But it's to Crouch's credit that he has now gone a long way towards silencing the critics, both on the terraces and in opposition dug-outs, as he has developed into one of English football's most respected forwards, and a regular for both club and country.

Of course, his height gives him a distinct advantage in both penalty areas, but it's not just his aerial power that sets him apart. Indeed, there's no doubt that were he just 'a head on a stick', as one former team-mate once described him, then he would not have cost an aggregate of almost £16 million in transfer fees; he would not be playing for one of the biggest clubs in Europe; and he would certainly not be an integral member of his country's international squad.

For his part, the abuse – or 'stick' as he prefers to refer to it – is water off a duck's back. 'You've got to have a sense of humour,' he told the *Daily Express*. 'If I took what people said about me to heart, there's no way I could be a footballer. You can't take yourself too seriously. A lot of people do, but I don't. It's got me this far, so I won't be changing.

'Everyone's entitled to their opinion. But for every person who is anti-you, there's someone who's for you. If you want to play at the highest level, you have to accept criticism. There have been times when it has been hard, but you can't take yourself too seriously.

'I know I am not your average-looking football player and I never will be. And I can understand why it is an issue for other people, why there are divided opinions about me. Certain people think I am a great player, others do not. And I will probably always be trying to prove a point to those people because of the way I look. But I see that as just one of those things. I am certainly comfortable with the way I am.

'My attitude is that if you start worrying about any of that stuff then you will not be able to play at this level. I am just getting on with it.'

And he's getting on with it to thoroughly good effect. After all, the likes of Rafael Benitez, Sven-Goran Eriksson, Steve McClaren, Harry Redknapp and Graham Taylor can't all be wrong; each of them has either backed or bought Peter Crouch at various stages of his career.

Former and current team-mates also talk animatedly about his assets and his value to a team, and they would have nothing to gain by publicly singing his praises while privately slagging him off. As anyone who has spent any time around footballers will know, if they think someone is not good enough or if they are not performing, they are not afraid of making their opinions heard.

That he appears to retain the support of his playing colleagues even when things are not going well – as was the case during his first season at Liverpool when he endured a lengthy 19-game goal drought at the start of his Anfield career – speaks volumes for the kind of character he is. Even his former boss at Aston Villa, David O'Leary, a man who clearly did not rate him as a player, described Crouch as 'a lovely big bag of bones'.

But, while Crouch is happy to be one of football's Mr Nice Guys, perhaps his determination to be so is to his own detriment; his own manager, Benitez, says of him, 'He's a nice boy and sometimes he's too nice. As a centre-forward in England, you must not be nice.'

However, off the pitch, there is steel and determination running through his wiry frame.

While not one to argue openly with his manager, he insists, 'I don't know what he meant, to be honest. Too nice? You can be a nice person off the field, but as soon as you get on the pitch you have to change, you have to be aggressive. I think I am.

'I know it has been said, but, when I go on the pitch, it's not "after you". I think you can be as nice as you like off the pitch, but when you get on it, you can't be nice, you've got to change your personality and thankfully I can do that,' he told the *Sunday Times*.

'I can be ruthless, I can be aggressive … but you don't have to go home and be aggressive with your missus. You can change. I know inside how much things matter to me, how much I want it. Maybe it doesn't come across at times, but I've got a strong desire to succeed. Maybe because I'm not so emotional, people don't see it, but I assure you it's there. I've always been a person who doesn't show too many feelings to people. I relay some things, but a lot of things I keep to myself.'

But surely some of the crowd abuse must hurt?

'You get the odd idiot,' he admitted in the same interview. 'But the good points about being a footballer far outweigh the bad. Stick's part and parcel. I've been on certain terraces myself when I was younger, dishing it out. There are a lot of witty people in football crowds and sometimes you'll hear something that makes you stop and laugh even if it's directed at you.

'I've always liked banter. My mates at home, we take the mickey as much as any group of lads. Just when I think I've heard every gag in the book regarding height, they come up with a new one and make me laugh.

'Everyone's entitled to their opinion. It would be easy to shy away and say, "Oh no, don't hurt me," but I'm not like that. If you want to play at the highest level, you have to accept criticism. Being so obvious, I'm an easy target, but it's not a problem. You've got to laugh. If you didn't laugh, you'd cry.'

But Crouch does confess that the flak he receives upsets his family – dad Bruce, mum Jayne and sister Sarah – more than it does him.

'I brush it all off but my dad is a different character. Any parent would react,' he continued. 'If someone's hammering their son, they're going to take it to heart, and, if someone gives me a bit of stick, he takes it worse than I do.

'I owe Mum and Dad everything. They took me everywhere when I was younger and are at every game. The stick must have hurt. I'm sure it wasn't nice for them.'

Dad Bruce later admitted to the *Daily Express*, 'We're delighted – not just because he is getting to the top of his profession, but because he has done it the hard way. His height has made it a struggle and I believe he's had to fight harder because of it.'

Peter's mum, Jayne, added in the *Sunday Mirror*, 'I just wish people would stop going on about how tall he is, as if he is some kind of freak. I'm always upset by people going on about Peter's height. They don't do it to the short players. He isn't some freakish giant; he's our son and his height has nothing to do with his football.

'I think it diverts attention away from his huge talent.

Just because Peter is 6ft 7in, people should not treat it as a sideshow.'

* * * * * * *

Crouch has been proving people wrong throughout his career, although the one man who he was not able to win over was then Aston Villa boss O'Leary, who clearly didn't rate him and offloaded him to Southampton.

But even on the south coast he initially found himself out in the cold after Paul Sturrock was sacked and Steve Wigley replaced him. Only when Harry Redknapp took over from Wigley did the ugly duckling truly begin to flourish into a swan. The rest, as they say, is history.

Harry Redknapp's son, Jamie, later wrote in a newspaper column in the *Daily Mail*, 'When my dad, Harry, became the manager at Southampton, Peter Crouch had not started a game all season. They would not have got £200,000 for him.

'Yet, after the first training session, Dad called and said, "I think I might have a player here; the kid can play. I might even be able to build a team around him."

'Two weeks later, I signed for the club and I could soon see why. By the end of the season, he was heading to Liverpool for £7 million.

'In training, he can do all the tricks. Like the rollover, the sort you'll see from Ronaldinho. Peter can manipulate the ball in a way that only a terrific technician can. His only "crime" is to be 6ft 7in.

'You can't be racist or homophobic, but you can poke fun at a tall guy and call him a freak. He has certainly changed some opinions.

'Aston Villa had become so uninterested in Peter that he'd been loaned out to Norwich in the Championship, where he scored four goals in 14 games alongside Darren Huckerby. He did all right there, but nothing more.

'Norwich had the money to buy one player, so they signed Huckerby and sent Peter back to Villa Park. Southampton signed him soon after, but they didn't know how to use him until Dad got hold of him. He scored on his first game back in the team against Middlesbrough and his confidence soared. Suddenly, he started to dominate defensive strongmen such as Ledley King, Sol Campbell, Kolo Toure, Gareth Southgate and Sami Hyypia.

'Dad would stand in front of the dressing room and say, "This man is going to win the game today, get the ball up to him," and you could see Peter grow in confidence. Before then, his shoulders were hunched.

'One afternoon, against Liverpool, he gave them such a chasing that Jamie Carragher called me after the game to say, "Can he play, or what?" We spoke regularly after that for the next four or five weeks and it soon became clear that Rafa Benitez was an admirer, too.

'Others started to take notice. Sammy Lee rang up before the [England] tour to America and asked me about him. He's not an Andy Gray or a Les Ferdinand in the type of headers he wins, but he can score with a guided header or cushion the ball down for a team-mate. It's not just about using him long, either. He'll come short and link the play. He's unselfish, he's comfortable receiving the ball in all areas of the pitch and he's also a force when defending set plays.

'When defending against him, what do you do? You must jump with him, but you won't win the ball. As a team defending against him, you must win the second ball.

'He's had to work so hard to change opinion; he's earned respect and he's not perceived as a joke figure any more. He's so much better than that. He can handle pressure; he can handle criticism. But can defenders handle him?'

Recent times have proved that many can't. It's also been proved that Crouch can handle just about anything and everything that is thrown at him.

'There have been plenty of ups and downs in my career,' he admits. 'But I never lost belief in my ability at any stage. I have good people around me who support me and the manager of England believes in me. Otherwise I wouldn't be playing. It is the same at Liverpool. The people who count have always believed in me.

'I am not the type of person to get down. I wouldn't say there have been many low moments. When I was at Aston Villa, there were difficult times, when you think you have done enough to play and you aren't. That was frustrating and it has definitely helped in my character and performance. You have to become hard and believe in yourself when others don't. Thankfully, I have done that and come out the other side.

'There have been times when it has been hard, but I've managed to get to a great club now and I feel I can enjoy playing for a great team. My job now is to go on and establish myself with England and Liverpool. It's called having the last laugh.

'When you have been relegated and been used to scrapping for every point, you appreciate it even more when you then get to play at this level. So I have been through a lot to get here. And I tell you what: I do not think anything can knock me down now.'

CHAPTER 1

EARLY DAYS

Peter Crouch was born on 30 January 1981 in Macclesfield, where his father, Bruce, was working as a junior advertising copywriter but, by the time he was five, his family had settled in Ealing, west London, via a year in Singapore.

It was in the Far East that he first showed an aptitude for football, with family photos showing him kicking a ball for the first time on a beach. It was a love affair that was to grow into the career he enjoys today.

Ironically, given the fierce rivalry these days between his current club and the one he followed as a youngster, Crouch was a boyhood Chelsea fan and used to stand in The Shed with his father and grandfather. Indeed, at the age of ten, he became a Stamford Bridge ball boy.

He was also keen on Queens Park Rangers, and posters of Kerry Dixon and Gordon Durie used to battle for space on his bedroom wall alongside those of Rangers' strikers Les Ferdinand and Roy Wegerle.

By that stage, he was already displaying signs of the talents that have made him the player he is today, starring for his school team at North Ealing Primary School, including one game where he scored a remarkable 13 goals!

His former teacher Phillip Wareing recalls those days with fondness. He told the *Ealing Times*, 'I remember Peter very well. He was always up for a laugh, and very popular with the other children.

'When I first saw him play football, I knew he had talent. He would score at least seven or eight goals a game for the school team. Sometimes we would put him in defence to give the others a chance. Once we even put him in goal – but he would come up for corners and still score.'

Ironically, given his current status as the tallest man ever to play for England, height was not his main asset in those primary-school days. 'He wasn't particularly tall at that stage,' added Wareing. 'People always talk about how tall he is and that he's a great header of the ball, but at age ten or eleven people don't head the ball, it's all on the floor.

'He was just great at holding it up, passing and scoring great goals.'

One crucial match during his formative years ended in tears rather than cheers, however, and provided a nasty pre-cursor of what was to come at the 2006 World Cup finals, when England's hopes were dashed once again during a penalty shoot-out.

On this occasion, it wasn't a shoot-out that was to blame, but a failure from the spot nonetheless. Wareing recalled, 'We got to the semi-finals of the borough schools league tournament in 1992. Peter missed a penalty in that match, which meant we lost, and he was devastated, crying and really upset.

'But, in the end, he was the player who had got us there almost single-handedly. We've never done that well since.'

Wareing has, naturally, continued to follow his former pupil's progress and is delighted to see how well he has done in the game. He added, 'I used to watch him playing for QPR and sometimes the abuse and ridicule he got from the stands was really bad, but Peter never let it get to him.

'He has always been the consummate professional, he never got cross. We are all totally behind him. We are very proud that he's come through the school.

'The kids get very defensive of him, and get cross if anyone says anything bad about him. They're all very loyal. They all love him – they think he's still part of their team.

'We all feel he deserves the success he's had. He was always a star to us, even when he played at QPR, but now he really is a superstar.'

From North Ealing Primary, Peter moved on to Drayton Manor High School, where he was known as 'Rodney' due to his resemblance to Del Boy's younger brother in *Only Fools and Horses*, and it was here that his genuine footballing ability was first noticed by a wider audience.

By now he had enjoyed a growth spurt and his PE

teacher back then, Paul Bowman, remembers that even in those early days the junior Crouch was never afraid to make the most of his physical attributes. Bowman recalled in the *Sunday Mirror*, 'Even as a pupil here Peter had a height advantage and used it. We're proud of what he has achieved.'

It was during those days playing for the school team that talent scouts from London's leading clubs first spotted his goal-scoring potential. He trained as a youngster at QPR, before following former Loftus Road boss Gerry Francis to Tottenham when he was 15. After passing ten GCSEs, Crouch was signed by Spurs when he left school at 17 but, despite his early promise, he failed to make the grade at White Hart Lane.

By then, in fact, he could have been lost to the game altogether. At 15, he was a promising tennis player and admits he was forced to make a choice between the two sports. He later told the *News of the World*, 'I played at county level. I had a big serve. Maybe I could have been the next Henman or Rusedski, but in the end it made more sense to choose football.'

But, when he found himself struggling at Tottenham and loaned out to non-league Dulwich Hamlet in 2000, he could have been forgiven for thinking he had made the wrong choice. Certainly, there was no suggestion then that he would go on to enjoy the successful career he has carved out for himself. Indeed, so ungainly was he during those days that he was rather cruelly nicknamed 'Bambi On Ice' by officials at the south London side.

He scored on his debut for the Ryman League outfit in a 2–1 win over Billericay Town, but failed to find the net in six subsequent appearances and the club rejected the opportunity to extend his one-month loan stay.

Chairman Martin Eede told the *Sunday Mirror*, 'Nobody at the club felt he had any chance of going on to be a top-class player. He was very tall, but was poor in the air and very ungainly – a bit like Bambi on ice. We never asked Spurs about extending his time with us because we had other strikers.'

Press secretary John Lawrence agrees with the chairman's assessment of the failed forward. He revealed in an article in the *Mirror*, 'He was a very nice lad and had no arrogance about him, despite him coming to us from Tottenham. He was down to earth, friendly and had quite a skilful touch.

'He certainly didn't celebrate with his robot dance, it was much more low-key than that. Never in a million years did we think he would end up playing for England.'

Crouch had a further loan spell during his time at Tottenham, this time to Sweden, where he played for minnows IFK Hassleholm. But he made a bigger impression in the bar than he did on the pitch!

Former team-mate Alexander Soderberg told the *Sun*, 'Of course I remember Peter. But frankly I must say he was better at drinking beer than playing football. I think he drank more beer than water during his time with us. But he was also very polite and a good friend.

'The funny thing is that he was not very good in the air despite his height. Actually, he became shorter when he tried to jump. But I must say that Peter was tremendous with his feet. To be that tall and have that kind of technique, that's something. It was amazing stuff because we thought it would take too long for his brain to connect with his feet because of his size.'

By the time Crouch returned to north London, Francis had left and it was clear that the new management team at Spurs – headed by George Graham and David Pleat – didn't rate him and that his days at White Hart Lane were numbered. In fact, he was struggling even to get a game for the club's reserve side.

Tottenham's first-team coach Chris Hughton later said in the *Evening Standard*, 'On the ground he had good feet and was quite a good finisher. As a young lad he didn't punch his weight in the air, but we were aware there was more to come from him.'

But Spurs were not prepared to invest any more time, or money, in the lanky front-runner and it appeared as though his boyhood dreams of a life as a professional footballer could be coming to an end before they had even started.

The striker later admitted to the *Evening Standard*, 'I have come through some hard times and there were times at Spurs when I wondered about the future, but I always knew I would make it. When you join a club like that you always hope that one day you will break into the first team. But it became clear to me that was never going to happen and I had to make decisions for the sake of my career.

'I always felt I could play at the highest level if I was given the opportunity, but George Graham and David Pleat were in charge then. I don't think they ever thought that I would make it. Leaving Tottenham was a huge wrench for me because I had been there so long as a kid and I had grown up with so many of the young stars there.

'I was behind lots of good strikers in Steffen Iversen, Sergei Rebrov and Les Ferdinand and, while I may have thought I could have done a better job than some of the reserve strikers who were ahead of me, it was still a wrench to make the decision to go. I took a lot of advice from coaches Chris Hughton and Pat Holland, but I realised, if I was to progress, I had to get away.

'I don't have anything to prove to them and I still have a lot of good friends there. But I was playing too much reserve-team football and I didn't think my career was progressing how I wanted it to and I had to get away to prove myself.'

And Francis, who by now had returned to Loftus Road as manager, was happy to grant the big striker his wish for a fresh start away from N17. Despite the west London club being perilously short of cash, Francis managed to raise a transfer fee of £60,000 and, in the summer of 2000, Crouch was on his way back to Shepherd's Bush. Who would have thought that just five years later he would join Liverpool for more than ten times that figure?

'David Pleat, their then manager, told me he didn't think Peter would make it there, so he was prepared to sell him,' remembered Francis in an interview with the *Sun*. 'I was delighted. I had that feeling that "I can make this boy a player".

'When David said we could have him. It was music to my ears. The feeling was the same as when I trekked down to St Blazey in Cornwall many years ago, and found a warehouseman playing in goal for £100 a week. I gave him £105 and took him to Bristol Rovers. He went on to become the first £1 million goalkeeper – it was Nigel Martyn.'

It was back at Loftus Road that Crouch's career finally began to blossom. Along with Francis, another key figure in his development was Des Bulpin, his former youth coach at Spurs who had followed Francis back to QPR as part of his backroom staff.

Bulpin had always rated Crouch, insisting even when he was a teenager that the gangly youngster would go on and play for England. But not everyone was so convinced by the young man who was already 6ft by the time he was 15.

And even at 19, on his return to Rangers, there were many who doubted whether he would make the grade in the professional ranks, let alone scale the heights. Francis remembers Crouch's first day at training following his transfer from Spurs.

'I remember the other players gawping when he came into training on the first day,' continued Francis. 'They were looking at each other and laughing. You knew what they were thinking. It was the same when he first arrived at Tottenham. I remember him walking across the pitch when he joined us at Spurs and people looked at him thinking, "What the hell is that? There's no way he can play, surely?" Well, you should never judge a book by its cover.

'It's what Peter has had to put up with ever since. He still does now but look at what he has achieved already. He takes the ribbing about his height in such good heart. That tells you a lot about the boy.'

Even so, Francis is man enough to admit that even he had reservations the very first time his path crossed that of the teenage Crouch. He confessed in the *Sun*, 'I must admit, when I first laid eyes on Peter, I thought "Jesus Christ!" just like everyone else does. His legs were a mile long and he looked as if a puff of wind would knock him over as he walked across the pitch.

'You couldn't miss him, even then. You could be forgiven for thinking, "How is this kid ever going to become a player? He hasn't got it in him." At the time he was signing YTS forms at Spurs we had to put him in extra large men's shorts because his legs were a mile long even then.

'People would take one look and think he couldn't play the game. Des [Bulpin] really believed in him, though. Peter had a good touch and we worked hard at building his strength so he wouldn't get knocked off the ball. He was intelligent, and when he jumped no one could touch him. He is not just tall, he has a good spring which is not always the case with tall people.'

One of those disbelieving new team-mates at Rangers was midfielder Matthew Rose, but it didn't take long before he and the other doubters had been converted to the Peter Crouch fan club.

'When Peter turned up we just saw him as a head on a stick,' said Rose in the *Mail on Sunday*. 'He got some terrible treatment from opposition defenders. They couldn't win a header against him so they were prone to bully him. I remember Darren Moore marking him against Portsmouth. Darren is a wily old customer and wasn't prepared to be out-jumped all afternoon so the first 50/50 ball he hammered into Crouchy and tried to put him into row Z.'

Francis had intended to ease Crouch into the first team

gradually, but an injury to first-choice striker Rob Steiner – and no money to sign a replacement – meant the teenager was thrust in at the deep end.

He made his league debut on the first day of the 2000–01 season in a 0–0 draw at home to Birmingham and went on to play 42 games that season, scoring ten goals.

The first of those goals came against Gillingham in September 2000 in a 2–2 draw at Loftus Road. Crouch's strike came just 21 minutes after he had come on as a substitute, replacing midfielder Steve Morrow, and it had extra significance as it was Rangers' first as they set about clawing back a two-goal deficit. For good measure, he then created the equaliser for strike partner Chris Kiwomya seven minutes before the end of the game.

Gillingham goalkeeper Vince Bartram remembers the game, and Crouch, well. He later told the *Independent*, 'I remember seeing some pre-season footage of him and thinking, "He's a big lad, a bit out of the ordinary." He came on with us 2–0 up and cruising. He scored their first goal – a very, very good volley – and then set up the second.

'As a keeper playing against a team with someone who is 6ft 7in, or any good header of the ball, the manager will say, "Come for crosses, help your defenders out." It means you have to be more positive and that can lead to mistakes because you are taking risks.

'Even then he did not get the respect he deserved for his technical ability. With some big men you can think, "We'll let them have possession as they won't cause any problems," but Crouch will.'

By this time, his Rangers' colleagues had long since changed their opinion of the big striker. 'We realised this was no head on a stick,' added Rose in the *Mail on Sunday*. 'I'd started at Arsenal and Peter reminded me of Alan Smith, who was tall and good in the air, but who was also able to bring the ball down and score goals.

'But there was still some fun poked at Peter because of his height. We had a poster of a skeleton in the physio's room and someone scrawled "Crouchy" all over it!'

However, behind the smiles, the club was in turmoil. In desperate financial trouble and with relegation looming, manager Francis resigned in February 2001. It was a genuine thunderbolt for the young Crouch.

He later said in an interview with the *Evening Standard*, 'I will always be grateful to Gerry and Des Bulpin. They were big influences on my career. Gerry was working with the first team at the time so it was Des who worked hard with me in those early days. He believed in me. He alerted Gerry to me and I have a lot to thank him for. He gave me my debut at QPR, he had faith in me in that first season and I managed to score a few goals. It was a great platform for me and a great start to my career.'

Francis remembers his former star pupil with similar affection. In his interview with the *Sun*, he added, 'Peter will never be a problem to manage. He is not built that way, to cause problems and unrest. But it would be fair to say that he is the sort of player who needs an arm around him. He needs his manager to believe in him, because he gets so much stick. We had to do it at QPR, partly because we threw him into the old Division One against tough men when he was just eighteen.'

Former Rangers player Ian Holloway was brought in to try to steady the ship after Francis's departure, but by then it was too late and the club dropped into the old Second Division (now League One).

And at the end of that season, and with the club in administration and desperate to cut costs – having informed the players that their salaries would be slashed ahead of the forthcoming season – they agreed a £1.5 million fee with Portsmouth for Crouch.

Holloway was desperate to keep the striker, but could do nothing to prevent him leaving for the south coast. 'Just 13 games I had with Crouchy,' he told *The Guardian*. '"Wrench" isn't the word for losing him. After the season had finished, David Davies, our chief executive, called me and said there was an offer of £1.5 million from Portsmouth for Crouchy. I said that he should turn it down, that he was worth £4–5 million.'

But Davies had no alternative but to accept the offer. However, that wasn't the end of Holloway's involvement in the deal. To his amazement, he discovered there was no sell-on clause in the contract, and he actually rang Crouch to intervene and insist on its inclusion.

Holloway continued, 'I rang Peter and told him, "This can't go through." Of course, it kicked off with Portsmouth, but I stood fast and said there would have to be a 15 per cent sell-on. I said to Crouchy, "Do you think it's fair to let you go without a percentage?" He said no and, in fairness to Peter, he phoned Harry Redknapp at Portsmouth himself and told him the deal would be off if they didn't agree to it.'

It was an extraordinary gesture on behalf of the player, to put the stricken club's interests before his own. 'There are not many players who would do that, but that's

Crouchy, he's different class,' adds Holloway. 'He and his dad, Bruce, are like that: there's nothing selfish about them. The most important thing about him [Crouch] is that he's a real person. In this hectic world where the players are often getting paid too much, he's a bit of sanity. I told his dad that the way Crouchy had behaved himself spoke volumes about his upbringing.'

Crouch, himself, is quick to recognise the part played by his parents in his football development. Although his father has a high-powered advertising career, they were always there for their son's matches – and still are – and would drive him around for training and games.

In fact, when Peter was injured at 14 while playing for the QPR youth team, it meant he couldn't do his early-morning paper deliveries. But, rather than see him lose his round, Bruce would get up at 5.30 a.m. and drive around Ealing delivering the papers. He had to start so early because at the time he was creative director of a leading UK company and had to be at his desk by 8 a.m.!

'I owe Mum and Dad everything,' said Crouch in an interview with the *Sunday Times*. 'They took me everywhere when I was younger and are still at every game.'

In those early days of his league career, though, Bruce's passion to see his son succeed nearly got him into trouble. After all, Crouch has had to put up with verbal abuse from opposition fans throughout his career, but it was far more vitriolic at the start of his career.

Crouch recalls one game at Gillingham where his dad actually had to leave the ground before doing something he would later regret, as he had to sit and listen to the vigorous abuse directed towards his son. Peter continued in the *Sunday Times*, 'To be fair, Dad's got a temper on him. He's learned to curb it, but when I first started and someone said something in the crowd, I wouldn't say he'd beat them up, but he'd have a few stern words. He's 6ft 5in and 15st, a big lad, but he's had to mellow.'

The memory of some of those games in the lower reaches – and the days of making ends meet on a pittance compared to his salary today – makes Crouch appreciate all the more what he's got now.

'At the start of my career I drove an old green Polo and the lads gave me some stick – because I couldn't fit into it, probably! It was all I could afford and I thought I was lucky. Then I had a Renault Megane for a while. I thought I was top man with that!'

But, while the stick he got from his mates was all good-natured, it was less friendly on a cold, wet Wednesday at somewhere like Grimsby. 'At least in the Premiership, when you've got 60,000 people screaming at you, you block the noise out,' he added in the *Sunday Times*. 'It was worse in Division One when you had one man and a dog watching. You'd go past them and be able to hear every word of abuse the bloke's giving you. It wasn't pleasant.'

Not pleasant, maybe, but it prepared the young Crouch well for the challenges, and the criticism, that lay ahead.

CHAPTER 2

LIFE ON THE SOUTH COAST

Had it not been for one ill-advised telephone conversation and one man's faith in his ability to succeed, Peter Crouch's career could have been very different.

Shortly before his move to QPR in the summer of 2000, Crouch was actually due to go on a loan spell to Barry Town. The then Barry boss Peter Nicholas, a former Welsh international midfielder, had agreed with David Pleat, Tottenham's director of football, to take the teenage striker on a three-month stint in South Wales.

Nicholas had only been in charge at Jenner Park for a matter of weeks and needed a striker for his club's forthcoming Champions League qualifier against Portuguese side Boavista. It was for this reason he got in touch with Pleat.

Nicholas explained to the *Western Mail*, 'I knew David Pleat very well as I played for him at Luton. After taking over at Barry, I rang him to say we were about to play Boavista in the Champions League and I needed a striker. He said, "No problem, you can have the boy Crouch on a three-month loan."

'He knew what a terrific experience it would be for Peter to play in the Champions League at such a young age – how many 19-year-olds get to do that? I was thrilled to get Crouchy because I'd known Peter since he was 13 when I used to see him on the youth circuit in London.

'Even when I used to watch him playing youth-team football then, I knew one day he'd be a star. His size is astronomical, isn't it? And his touch, for someone so tall, is excellent. You don't often find a big centre-forward who also has a good touch. He's not a bully of a striker – just brainy. I knew he'd be an asset to us because of his height and his ability on the ball.

'Anyway, as Peter was driving down from London, I had a phone call from a friend of mine called Des Bulpin, who was assistant manager to Gerry Francis at QPR. A bit naively, I said to Des, "You'll never guess who I've managed to sign – Peter Crouch." He said, "You're joking?"

'I should've realised I was shooting myself in the foot because Des also knew Peter very well, of course. Anyway, half an hour later, as I'm waiting for Peter to arrive, I get a call to say Crouch won't be coming to Barry after all as, in that short space of time, QPR had done a deal with Spurs to sign him.

'And that was that – we'd missed out on Crouch because of me letting the cat out of the bag on the phone to Des. Peter was our man for about three hours – that's the length of time that elapsed between Spurs agreeing to let him come to us on loan and QPR taking him off our hands.

'Every time I see him on the telly playing for Liverpool or England now I think back to the time I almost got him down to Barry.

'I couldn't blame him for going to QPR. We'd been so close to getting him. At least it showed my judgement was good! What can you do? I went off to sign Jamie Moralee (the former Millwall striker) instead. The rest is history, I suppose.'

So, instead of South Wales, it was in west London that Crouch continued his football education. His impressive first season of league football was enough to convince Portsmouth to pay cash-strapped QPR £1.5 million for him and, at just 20, Crouch found himself on the move again, this time to the south coast and to his third club in a little over a year in his fledgling career. Once more, however, it would turn out to be a brief coupling between player and club.

Not that things went badly for Crouch at Portsmouth. Far from it. He was an unqualified success at Fratton Park and that, more than anything, ensured that the relationship would be a short-lived one.

In fact, to all intents and purposes, it was a marriage made in heaven from day one. Or certainly from day one of the Football League season at any rate.

Portsmouth were handed a tough-looking trip to Molineux to take on Wolves, a trip made all the more difficult by the tragic death of their goalkeeper, Aaron Flahavon, in a car crash the weekend before. Under those circumstances, it would have been easy for the players to hide, but it took Crouch just eight minutes to break his Pompey duck with a superb downward header past Michael Oakes to ease the gloom – if only marginally. The game eventually finished 2–2, so, although Crouch did not get the debut victory he or the other players would have wanted, he could feel well satisfied with his own contribution.

Manager Graham Rix spoke afterwards of a tough seven days at the club, saying, 'It has been a traumatic week. The players were emotionally drained and I am proud of them all. I told them we had to go out and do it for Flav.'

He had made a fantastic start for his new club, a start he was to build on in fine style. He was on target again in his third match, scoring Pompey's only goal in a disappointing 2–1 home defeat at the hands of Colchester United as they crashed out of the League Cup at the first hurdle. Then, in his fifth game, he really showed the Fratton Park crowd what he could do in a Portsmouth shirt.

The late August Bank Holiday Monday in 2001 saw Grimsby visit the south coast, and Rix was able to field his 'dream' front pairing of Crouch and new signing Mark Burchill, the former Celtic striker, for the first time. And how well they played together.

The pair both scored twice in a 4–2 victory and it appeared as though Portsmouth would be well set for a promotion challenge in the months to follow. Rix was delighted, saying after the game, 'They are two very different players, but they've shown what they can do and I'm looking forward to seeing them play together for the rest of the season. We have a first-class strike partnership now and I think they are going to cause defences in the First Division a lot of problems.'

The goals continued to flow for the duo in the next few weeks – 3–3 v. Wimbledon (a goal apiece), 4–2 v. Crystal Palace (again, a goal apiece) – and a genuinely threatening partnership, one that would strike fear into the division's defences, looked to be blossoming.

Portsmouth moved into second place in the table following that victory over Palace and there was a real feeling of optimism around the town that maybe this was to be their season. The fans were happy, and so too was the club management. Rix said at the time, 'They are such a young team but they are all desperate to play for the shirt and are very eager and enthusiastic.

'They will make mistakes along the way but there is still a lot better to come from them and the difference now is that we look like scoring every time we go forward.'

However, a hugely unfortunate training-ground accident towards the end of September was to burst the bubble, and almost certainly put paid to Portsmouth's hopes of sustaining a genuine challenge among the leaders. In fact, from then on, amid fans' protests and boardroom frustration, it was a story of gradual decline.

Former Fratton Park coach Jim Duffy later told the *News of the World*, 'We thought the mix of Burchy's acceleration and Crouchy's touch and ability in the air would work well for us, and it did. I think in the first six or seven games they played together that season they both scored four or five goals.

'The combination was shaping up well until one day in training Burchy clipped Robert Prosinecki's heel. It opened his knee up and he did his cruciate ligaments. It was a freak accident but it set Burchy back for two years, really. I felt that if the two of them had stayed together we would have made the play-offs.'

As it was, Portsmouth ended the season in a disappointing 17th place, 22 points below those play-off spots. The lowest point came in February 2002, when chairman Milan Mandaric stopped the players' wages, and those of manager Rix, following a 5–0 defeat at West Bromwich Albion.

The players provided an immediate response, winning their next game against Coventry, leaving the Pompey chief feeling vindicated in his decision. Mandaric insisted, 'The wages are paid from my personal account because, without me, the club is insolvent. But this is not about the money, it's about principle. The performance against Coventry proves what these players can achieve if they put some effort into it.

'They have constantly underachieved all season. The performances this season lead me to wonder just why I am paying some of them extortionate wages. These players earn thousands a week, and the great supporters in this city, who fork out hard-earned wages, deserve better. If the players were in any other industry, they would be held accountable for their results and performance at work by their employer. Therefore, as their employer, I am doing the same.'

Rix himself said after the victory over Coventry, 'The players had a choice. I told them before the match, "If you want to see me on Wednesday morning, you'd better win tonight."'

Despite the upheaval at the club, however, the campaign was a personal triumph for Crouch. He netted 18 goals in 37 league matches at a strike rate of more than a goal every other game.

Not that that goals return came as a surprise to Duffy, who continued in the *News of the World*, 'I was in charge of Chelsea's youths under Luca Vialli, and the kids on our side knew all about Crouchy. When we played Tottenham, they told me that, in spite of his exceptional height, the plan would be to play the ball to his feet instead of his head.

'Right away I could see good balance and a lovely first touch. If he was 5ft 9in tall, nobody would remark on how good he is with the ball at his feet. But his height gets in the way of people's appreciation of him.

'I christened him the "baby giraffe" because his legs didn't seem to match up with the rest of his body, but he reminded me of a young Tore Andre Flo in the way he drifted away from the usual centre-forward's position to do his damage.

'He knew from an early age that defenders would try to bully him and that increased his awareness of how to cause them problems by not allowing anyone to get in front of him when he received the ball.'

Duffy continued to follow Crouch's progress but, while he always liked what he saw of him, he is quick to point out that, in actual fact, it was Rix who persuaded the Portsmouth board to invest in the striker.

'I have to hold my hand up and say it was Graham Rix who signed him for Portsmouth,' admitted Duffy in the same interview. 'He was convinced about him, whereas I still had my doubts. I knew he had ability, but I didn't know whether he'd be physically strong enough, because at that time the Championship was [physically] tougher than the Premiership and Peter was only 20.

'The other point was that the chairman, Milan Mandaric, had been asking us about bringing in players who could be profitably sold on. Milan felt we were missing out a wee bit, so we went for two young guys – Peter and Burchy.

'We felt that if Peter did well he'd get a move for good money, and that's what happened. He came for £1.5 million in July and left for £5 million the following March, so Milan was quite happy!

'Peter's biggest asset was definitely his touch. Everyone looked at him and thought "target man", but he had a unique way of playing because he had ability and he was so big.

'He's had to turn everyone around throughout his career, though. He's always had to listen to people saying he should have been a basketball player, but he has the personality that just smiles through it all.

'He's got a great personality and he was popular with the other players. He was very relaxed and he didn't take himself too seriously. He was one of those guys you hoped would have a good career because he was so likeable. But, inside, he's shown some real strength of character.'

Former Pompey team-mate Scott Hiley also rates Crouch highly and, like Duffy, wasn't shocked by how well he did during his one season at Fratton Park. 'I'd seen him in a reserve game for Tottenham, so I knew what to expect,' he said in the *Independent*. 'He doesn't look like a footballer. He's very ungainly and people assume he can't be any good. But when you get the ball at his feet he's different class.

'He was a handful in training. He doesn't just stand there. He jumps, too. That makes it even worse. We had great joy with him. We had two decent wingers, so he was scoring goals and laying them on.

'For a full-back like me he was a fantastic target. He was always available and you could fire it in at any height because his control was exceptional. He was easy to find and the ball tended to stick. But he's more than just a target man, he can link play.

'He's a lovely lad. He joined in the banter, but didn't get any stick in the dressing room. He was getting enough from the other fans with all these chants of "freak", so we weren't going to add to it.'

A recurring theme whenever people talk about Crouch is how well liked he was at every club he's played for; how courteous and appreciative he was of the help being given to him, both by the coaching staff and his fellow players. But, while that mild-mannered nature might be considered a weakness in some quarters, Crouch has no qualms about being as vociferous as the next man when he feels the situation warrants it.

And he had cause to voice his opinion on several occasions throughout the season as the pressure continued to mount on the under-fire Rix. 'The players have to take the blame,' Crouch told reporters at the time. 'It was Graham who brought me to Portsmouth and he has helped transform the fortunes of the club, which for seven or eight seasons has struggled to avoid relegation.

'I can't believe the pressure on him just because we've lost a few games. All the players are right behind him and it wouldn't be right if he were to go. He is the best man for the job.'

And it seemed as though he would perhaps be given more time to get things right at Portsmouth when the club secured their First Division status with six games to go following a draw at Crewe. Rix said after that match, 'Every manager is under pressure, but there's no extra pressure on me at this club. We are safe with six games to go, so as far as I'm concerned that's progress for Portsmouth.'

Despite his bullish attitude, however, the writing was on the wall for Rix and it was no real surprise when he was sacked in March 2002, 13 months after succeeding Steve Claridge in the job.

Mandaric said, 'It has been a difficult season which has not met my expectations or those of most of our supporters. I've been very patient and wanted Graham Rix to be successful, but the team has been very inconsistent and results have not been there.'

Veteran goalkeeper Dave Beasant was not so sure of the decision, however, insisting, 'We felt the team was going in the right direction. You'd have thought Rix would have been given until the end of the season.'

Harry Redknapp, the club's director of football, was appointed as the new manager, and one of the first decisions he made was to end the Portsmouth career of Crouch – accepting a £5 million bid from Aston Villa.

He said, 'Every player has his price and £5 million is a lot of money. Sometimes in football you have to make financial decisions. We're heading for losses of around £6 million this season and the chairman can't keep on putting his hand in his pocket.'

As for the former management team, they were left to reflect on what might have been. 'We got Peter Crouch for £1.5 million and sold him for £5 million to Aston Villa ten months later,' reflected Duffy in the *News of the World*. 'We would have got an award from the business community for that kind of profit, but in football it gets you the sack!'

CHAPTER 3

BECOMING A VILLAIN

Almost within hours of Harry Redknapp's appointment as Portsmouth boss, Peter Crouch was packing his kit bag once more and heading out of a club's 'exit' door for the final time. This time his journey was to take him to the Midlands, and his fourth club in under two years.

Having proved himself at First Division level in struggling sides at QPR and Portsmouth, he had every reason to approach the step up to the Premiership with confidence. After all, playing at a big club like Aston Villa, with better players, could surely only improve his game.

He, for one, certainly didn't lack confidence as he approached the task ahead after signing his four-year contract. 'I'm glad to be back with a Premiership club,' he said. 'I've always believed in my ability and that I would again return to a Premiership club after my early days with Tottenham.

'I didn't really think it was going to happen so quickly and it is an unbelievable feeling for me, and I am looking to repaying the faith Villa have shown in me. I've had two seasons in the First Division and now I'm desperate to prove myself in the Premiership. If I am half as successful as I was with Portsmouth then I will be very happy.

'I have to pay credit to [former manager] Graham Rix, who was a major influence on my career at Portsmouth. Personally, I'm just looking forward to playing in a successful side and scoring as often as I can for Villa, who are a massive club.

'I am aware that Graham Taylor's successes as a manager have come with a tall player up front, but I am my own man, my own player, and I don't like to be compared to anyone else. There are similarities to certain players, but I'd like to think I can bring something different to the side.'

His new manager, meanwhile, was thrilled at finally landing his man after having spent more than 18 months on his trail. And a measure of just how highly he rated Crouch was that the £5 million fee was the most Graham Taylor had paid for a single player in all his years in management.

The former England boss, who had nurtured the careers of other giant strikers, like Ross Jenkins, George Reilly and Ian Ormondroyd, has since revealed that he first tried to sign Crouch during his second spell in charge at Watford.

He told the *Sun*, 'I wanted to buy him for Watford. Peter was at QPR at the time and they were asking £1 million for him. Watford couldn't find the money, but it didn't deter me. What got me was that we had Elton John at Watford at the time, and Mike Sherwood of Goldman Sachs. The *Sunday Times* had just printed their rich list of the 300 wealthiest people in the country and both were in it. Yet the directors told me they couldn't afford £1 million!

'We then played QPR in the autumn of the season Watford went on to win promotion to the Premiership. We beat them and, as the players trooped off, I waited for Peter to come by, head hanging because he had lost. I thought, "I'm going to have this lad." I waited and waited. As he walked past I sidled up and whispered, "Big man, you can play. You're a player."

'His reaction was one of surprise, especially as QPR had just been beaten. But he was pleasantly surprised and he smiled before thanking me. I make no bones about it, I was tapping him up. Let's face it, we're all guilty of it. But I was determined to get him.'

And get him he eventually did, although not, of course, at Vicarage Road. And to the doubters who still appeared sceptical about Crouch's ability to cut the mustard at the very highest level, Taylor was adamant in his opinion that his judgement would be proved correct.

He insisted, 'Don't be fooled by Peter's height. When you are as tall as Peter, it's not easy for other people to recognise his level of skill. But I've got great confidence in his ability as a footballer. I have no problems about signing him and I hope he will be a huge success here.'

Crouch's move to Villa Park came at the end of an incredible week for the striker. Not only had he swapped the lower reaches of the First Division for the top ten of the Premiership in a £5 million transfer, he had also made his England Under-21 debut. Little wonder he described it at the time as 'the most unbelievable few days of my life'.

His first appearance in an England shirt at that level came on 3 March 2002, when he appeared as a second-half substitute against Italy at Bradford's Valley Parade. The stage was set, it appeared, for Crouch to make a real impact for both club and country.

Dad Bruce was hoping so. 'The one thing Peter has craved above anything else is the chance to play with top-class players,' he revealed to the *Sunday Mercury*. 'Peter is convinced that the better the team he is playing in, the more he will score and the better he'll get. Playing alongside the likes of Paul Merson, George Boateng and Darius Vassell at Villa, he's convinced he will only get better.

'And he will fit in, no trouble. He is used to handling pressure – he's been watched by half a dozen Premiership sides at every home game for most of the season and he's kept on scoring regardless.'

While Crouch's father was expecting his son to improve alongside the likes of Vassell, for his part the Villa striker was looking forward to linking up with a new strike partner. Just a day after Crouch won his first cap for the England Under-21s, Vassell had picked up his second full cap against Italy at senior level.

And he was relishing the opportunity of reuniting a pairing that first showed signs of promise during their days together in the national team's junior ranks. Vassell told the *Birmingham Post*, 'I am looking forward to getting the chance to play again alongside Peter having played with him a couple of times for the England Under-18 side.

'He's got a good goal-scoring record this season. Probably most people will call it the "Little and Large" show [Vassell is just 5ft 7in, to Crouch's 6ft 7in], but he is a good signing for Villa. It's always nice to have a new signing and we are all looking forward to what we can achieve under Graham Taylor.'

That endorsement was backed up by Crouch's former England Under-21 boss Peter Taylor, who reckoned Villa had signed a player good enough to follow Vassell from the Under-21s into the full England squad.

'Graham's made a good move there,' Peter Taylor told the *Sunday Mercury*. 'Peter is an excellent player, very skilful and someone who will score goals. People might look at him and wonder whether he is the real thing because of his size. He may be 6ft 7in, but he's good on the ground and very difficult to get the ball off. He can only improve, it's all there, and I can see him becoming an England regular at some stage, maybe in the next couple of years.'

Graham Taylor wasted no time throwing Crouch into the fray with his new team, pitching him straight into the side to face Bolton, basing his reasoning for that decision on the fact that 'I feel the adrenaline is still very high after a hectic week.'

He added, 'All of the clubs above us have a combination that can score goals. Every successful team will have not just one goalscorer, they will have two and the one thing that is pretty obvious to everybody is that we haven't been able to produce that.

'Now I'm hoping that Peter will give us other options and perhaps, among the strikers we've got, we'll find a partnership that looks as if it's going to score goals. There's no doubt about it, and it's silly trying to argue anything differently, that's been the biggest problem we've had all season – and perhaps in previous years, as well. We just haven't been able to find a partnership that can score.

'I'm hoping that with the different qualities Peter will bring to the strikers I have available, that perhaps between them now we can find a partnership that we can rely upon to score in a regular fashion.'

And so it was that Crouch made his Villa, and Premiership, debut on 30 March 2002 at Bolton's Reebok Stadium. It was something of an irony that Crouch should make his top-flight bow against Wanderers, as their manager, Sam Allardyce, was another admirer who had previously tried to sign him.

The Bolton boss revealed on the eve of the game, 'We know him well from his time at QPR and he has made great strides. I wanted to sign him, but we didn't have the funds. I felt that the price he went to Portsmouth for, with add-ons, was a very good price for a young player of his capabilities.

'He is an ungainly type of player who the fans probably wouldn't have taken to initially. But he would have won them over because of the goals he would have scored. "The next Niall Quinn" is an ideal tag for him. I think he is exactly that. He caused us an awful lot of problems last season. He is good on the ground, too. And he's not slow either. So we do know plenty about him. I'd say he was a shrewd investment by Graham Taylor.'

Crouch's first game in a Villa shirt didn't exactly go to plan as his new side went down 3–2, but he showed enough signs to suggest that he belonged in that sort of company. And, three days later, he really made his mark.

He celebrated his home debut with Villa's goal in a 1–1 draw against Newcastle United and, if he needed any encouragement as to how much hard work there was ahead for him, he needed only to look at the opposing centre-forward for inspiration.

It was Alan Shearer who opened the scoring on that rainy night at Villa Park, notching up his 199th Premiership goal. Crouch, though, spoiled his celebrations, opening his account in the English game's highest echelon with an excellent header from Gareth Barry's pinpoint cross.

Taylor, though, was quick to highlight afterwards to the massed ranks of the media, who were perhaps not so familiar with Crouch's attributes, that he was more than just a 'head on a stick', to coin a phrase from Matthew Rose.

Taylor said, 'I'll be saying this for some weeks now I suppose, but he has a good touch. If anything, because he has not fully developed physically, one of his weaker areas is in the air.

'I was pleased with the way Peter played. He showed good touches and did very well. It doesn't matter if you're 5ft 6in or 6ft 6in if you're a good player – and Peter is.'

A couple of weeks later, in a 2–2 draw at Leicester, Crouch provided further evidence that he belonged in Premiership company. Although he didn't score in the match at Filbert Street, he turned in perhaps his best all-round display so far for Villa in a superb demonstration of the way a big man should lead the line of attack.

That display did much to silence the doubters who had questioned the wisdom of Taylor's £5 million outlay on the lanky striker. After the match, however, Crouch insisted that the barbs of his detractors only increased his willingness to make them choke on their words.

'I think it makes me more determined to prove them [the critics] wrong,' he insisted to the *Birmingham Post*. 'With people who know me and know how I play, it has never been a problem. Once I get on the pitch, people can see that I can play, and hopefully I can prove those critics wrong. It's nice to do so.

'I think when I signed, people looked at me and, obviously because I'm tall, they thought about the aerial threat. But I do like to prove to people that I can play on the floor as well and, hopefully in the games so far, I have shown them that. I just hope there are a few more goals to come before the end of the season and at the start of next season.'

One moment of skill against Leicester proved beyond all reasonable doubt that Crouch had the ability to match his inches. With one excellent touch, he created space and an opportunity for himself and was denied a second Villa goal only by Leicester keeper Ian Walker's fine save.

Taylor insisted, 'If Peter had scored that goal, you would certainly have been talking about it. He made the chance for himself with an absolutely superb piece of skill. I think Walker's got to be given great credit for the save, but it was a tremendous piece of skill that created the chance for him.

'More and more people will become aware of how good his feet are. You feed it into him and he leads the line well. The players here know that they've got a good centre-forward. If he develops – and give it another couple of years – people won't even be talking about his height. They will be talking about everything else.'

Crouch ended the season with another Villa goal in the club's final game of the season – a 3–1 win away at Chelsea – that helped earn them a place in that summer's InterToto Cup competition.

He headed home Steve Stone's 21st-minute cross for Villa's opener, and his strike partner Vassell added the second. And Taylor was delighted to see the partnership he had worked so hard to create starting to pay dividends.

He said, 'They are beginning to look quite formidable together. Peter has had a hand in almost every goal we have scored since he came here.'

Other people were also clearly starting to take notice of Crouch's talents. *The Times'* match report for the Chelsea game read, 'Darius Vassell, the sprightly poacher, we all know about. But it is Peter Crouch, bought for £5 million from Portsmouth, who is the really intriguing figure. This 6ft 7in cross between a preying mantis and Rodney Trotter may amuse opposing defences on first acquaintance, but it won't be long before he makes them take him extremely seriously.'

That goal at Stamford Bridge took his tally for Villa to two in seven games, a respectable enough return for a young man taking his first tentative steps in the big time.

But his terrific season, which had seen him establish himself as a genuine threat in the First Division with

Portsmouth and then make his big-money move to the Premiership, was not over yet. He was selected for the England Under-21 squad for the European Championship finals in Switzerland and, a week after ending the domestic campaign with a goal at Stamford Bridge, he was on the mark again for his country.

He scored the first goal in England's 2–1 victory over the host nation in Zurich to put them on their way to a crucial victory. Having won the free-kick himself outside the area, Crouch was in the right place at the right time to pick up the pieces after David Dunn's goal-bound effort had been deflected into his path and he drilled home his first international goal in his third game for the Under-21s.

He admitted after that match, 'It's been an unbelievable few months for me. To be honest, I didn't know I was going to be coming to the championships, and to be in the side for the first game was a proud moment for me, and obviously to get my first England goal was another proud moment.

'At one point in the season, I was playing for Portsmouth and it was touch and go whether we were going to get relegated or not. Obviously the move to Villa came about, which was a superb move to a massive club. I've really settled in there and I've also settled in with the Under-21s as well. It has been a massive change, but it has come about at the right time.'

Sadly for Crouch and his young England team-mates, they were unable to build on that promising start to the competition, losing their two remaining group matches to Italy and Portugal to crash out before the knockout stages.

But for Crouch it was another step in the right direction along his development path and provided further proof that he was capable of scoring goals in whatever company he found himself. He had every reason to feel pleased with himself after a remarkable 12 months, and must have believed that the future would bring only better times.

The next season, however, was to provide the confident young man with a horrible, and painful, reality check.

To say he had a nightmare time of it in his first full season at Villa would be a gross understatement. It was nothing short of an unmitigated disaster – both for club and player alike.

It started badly with defeat in the InterToto Cup semi-finals against Lille, with the team having got past FC Zurich in the previous round, and it then went from bad to worse. Perhaps it would have been different had Villa capitalised on their excellent 1–1 draw in the first leg in France and finished the job in the return at home. Instead, they slumped to a dismal 2–0 defeat.

Perhaps, too, the season would have been different for Crouch had he not seen his angled shot cleared off the line by Rafael Schmitz on the half-hour mark in that second-leg encounter with the teams deadlocked at 0–0. There was to be far more misery in the ensuing months.

Taylor reflected afterwards, in what would prove to be a prophetic assessment of the season ahead, 'The difficulty is I wanted to move us forward in the InterToto Cup, because it is a way into the UEFA Cup, but I also want to look at players, to look at different formations and to prepare us for a ten-month season. I don't think I can settle on one formation for every [opposing]

Premiership side; I don't think we're good enough to play just the one shape.'

Just three wins in their first 12 Premiership games suggested that Taylor's overview of his side's strengths were spot on. By that point in the season Crouch had been consigned to the bench after an eight-game run, including those four InterToto Cup matches, without a goal.

Since that time Taylor has reflected that the decision to drop Crouch was wrong. 'What perhaps I should have done was stuck with him. Against Liverpool on the first day he had chances, then Kasey Keller brought off two great saves at Tottenham; Peter Schmeichel did the same against Manchester City, he missed another couple, then, when we lost at Bolton, I visibly saw the confidence drain out of him.'

His demotion from the first team resulted in a frustrating campaign for the 21-year-old, as he was forced to spend much of the time watching others trying in vain to revive the club's fortunes. Taylor, though, while keen to shield his young striker from further criticism, never lost faith in him.

And when he got his chance of a first-team return, against Southampton in March 2003 with Dion Dublin out of action through suspension, Taylor spoke eloquently in support of his under-fire forward.

On the eve of the match at The Dell he told the press, 'Peter and I have had long talks. I have belief in Peter; he knows that. But I also know that he has had a very bad season in terms of putting the ball in the back of the net. Peter knows as well as I do that whatever happens between now and the end of the season and what happens next season could make him or break him as a Premiership player.

'I do feel some sympathy for him. At 6ft 7in, all of the taunts are there. And I don't believe that, now and again, they haven't hurt him. Taunts can catch you at the wrong moment and must hurt you. And this is a decent lad. This isn't a lad who doesn't care. But he has to understand that, as much as I would support him, it will all be down to what he does for himself. Nobody's going to be interested in me saying what a skilful player he is if he can't put the ball in the back of the net.

'I am having to take into account what the atmosphere is. You have got to be mentally strong yourself. This is not a criticism of supporters, but they can make or break you. Sometimes, if people take a dislike to a player, those people want to be proven right. In that case, the player in question has to do something extraordinary sometimes for the people to even acknowledge that a player is half-decent. I cannot afford to have that in this situation.

'I will stand by Peter, but he has to recognise what he is up against. He has been scoring at all levels – except for the first team. Many can see his good touch, but he needs the goals.'

As a former Portsmouth player, Crouch was guaranteed a hostile reception at The Dell and the match ended in more disappointment for the by-now dejected and downhearted striker. He could have opened the scoring from Vassell's cross, but completely missed his kick in front of goal, and he was also wide of the target with two other good opportunities.

Finally, with 20 minutes remaining, he was replaced by

Marcus Allback and could only watch from the bench as Southampton's Kevin Davies grabbed a last-minute equaliser to earn the home side a point.

After the match, however, Crouch cut a defiant figure. He said, 'The stick did not worry me and I know the goals will come. I believe in my ability and I am relishing the challenge. Look at James Beattie for Southampton and his form currently. He had a bad spell, but now he can't stop scoring.'

Villa boss Taylor also vowed to stick by his under-fire striker. He insisted, 'I will always keep faith with players who give their best and want to do well. That's my job. Peter missed three or four chances, but at least he was in position to miss them. He got into the box. He's having a very hard season, but people forget he's just a kid.

'But he must show the mental strength to stick at it. The fellow has got to be strong. There's nobody who doesn't hit a brick wall. He is only 21 and has ten more years to learn from it.'

Despite the words of bravado from both men, however, the reality was very different. And Crouch's miserable afternoon back on the south coast turned out to be his final appearance of what had been a dreadfully disappointing season; one that had seen him fail to score in 18 appearances for the club.

Crouch's personal misery was reflected by the team's overall performance that term as they finished in a lowly 16th spot, just three points above relegated West Ham. It was certainly not the campaign either the players or the supporters were expecting.

And for the manager, enough was enough – he resigned

just three days after the final game of the season, frustrated by the club's lack of progress and the board's unwillingness to speculate in the transfer market.

In a prepared statement, Taylor said, 'Contrary to what may be perceived, playing results are not the reason for my resignation and I had always believed that the season was going to be one of transition, particularly in respect of emerging young players.

'The structure of the club has to be looked at on and off the field. People have to be able to look at themselves and say it is time for a change. If you get things right at the top there is a good chance it flows down.

'Certain aspects of the club had to show an improvement and had to change if I were to remain as manager. I didn't come back for us to finish 16th and that is where I failed; I failed to deliver a team that satisfied the supporters.

'When I came back I took a lot of pressure off the board, but that's not why I came back, I came back to deliver a successful team and I failed to do that.

'I would, however, point out that modern football, with its well-publicised financial pressures, involves much wider issues than mere playing matters, and those are a major factor in my decision.'

For Crouch, the departure of the manager who had signed him, and backed him, came as another major blow after a season that had been a personal nightmare. It was a sobering experience for the young player.

It must have been a difficult summer as he reflected on a season of turmoil, both personal and collective, at Aston Villa. But he had overcome many hurdles to get where he had in his career and Crouch had no intention of giving up at the first sign of trouble.

Instead, he returned to pre-season doubly determined to confound the critics once more and prove that he had a significant role to play in reviving Villa's fortunes. His first task, of course, was to convince new manager David O'Leary that he was worthy of a place in his first-choice XI.

With the likes of Juan Pablo Angel, Guy Whittingham, Marcus Allback and Darius Vassell all providing competition for places up front, he knew it would not be easy, but he was determined to prove himself a success at the club.

As he returned to pre-season, he outlined his desire to convince his critics he had a future at the top level in an interview with the *Birmingham Evening Mail*. He said, 'I've come back determined to forget about last season. The change of manager means we're all starting from scratch and looking to impress David O'Leary.

'This could be my chance to get back into the first team and I've not lost any belief in my abilities. I want to prove a few people wrong. The start of pre-season has been good and the gaffer is getting really involved in the day-to-day training. He has very clear ideas on how he wants us to play and I aim to be a part of his plans.

'Everybody is looking to catch his eye and I'm no different. There is a lot of competition for places up front and my aim has to be to get one of those two shirts. It won't be easy, we have some quality strikers here, but I'll be giving it my best shot.

'It was a hard season for me last season. To be in and

out of the team was difficult and it was the first time in my career that I'd taken a backseat. I can handle the Premiership. I have no doubts about that and I'm going to put a bad season behind me.

'When I get another chance to prove myself, I'm going to grab it. With the quality of strikers we've got at this club, when you get a chance, you've got to take it. When it comes around, I'm hoping to do that. I've also sat back and learned from the likes of Dion Dublin, who came back into the side and did really well. He encouraged me throughout the season and helped me.

'Last year I didn't get that early goal and that would have maybe settled me down. I think it started to affect me, but I've learned and I think I'm a better player for that. So if I can get off the mark early on this year, I think that will make a difference. I know there's only one way to win over the fans and that's to score goals. I'm confident I can do that.'

However, Crouch was not given a chance by O'Leary to prove either that he could score goals, or that he could win over the fans. He was given just 13 minutes as a substitute in the first game of the season at his former club Portsmouth, by which time Villa were 2–0 down (they eventually lost 2–1).

He was not even in the 16-man squad for the first home game of the season against Liverpool and it was clear that the writing was on the wall for the big man. And when Norwich came in at the start of September wanting to take him on loan, Aston Villa agreed and Crouch found himself back in the First Division, less than 18 months after he thought he had left it behind for good.

However, the 22-year-old was determined to look at the positive aspects of the move, rather than dwell on the negative. He insisted, 'I can't wait to be starting games again. Norwich are a good side and this is a great opportunity to show what I can do. I'm aiming to score goals so I can then go back to Villa and carve out a future there. The gaffer has told me I'm part and parcel of his plans.'

He was, though, prepared to admit that things had gone stale at Villa after what had been a promising start to his career there. 'I've had an indifferent time so far at Villa,' he confessed. 'It was very stop-start last season. I only played the full 90 minutes three or four times and that's not good enough. It has been frustrating, but now I just want to play as many games as I can to get back on track.

'When I joined Villa from Pompey I thought it was the perfect stage for me. Hopefully it will turn out that way and I'll stay there for the rest of my career. I've made loads of friends there and everything's fine, except that I'm not in the first team.

'Certainly I'd like to think that I can still do a job for Villa. Hopefully, when I get back from my loan spell, things can improve for me and I can get back into the Villa side. Coming to Norwich will hopefully help me and I want to help them as well, but come the end of the three months, you never know what's going to happen.

'I've been in and out of the Villa team this season and last and I'm just really excited at the prospect of playing again. Norwich are a decent side so this is a good opportunity. It has been frustrating sitting on the sidelines. Hopefully, I can play the majority of the games for Norwich.'

At the time of the move, Villa boss O'Leary insisted that he saw it only as being a temporary separation, and certainly not a divorce. Indeed, he fully expected Crouch to return following his three months in Norfolk with a renewed hunger for the Premiership.

The Irishman said, 'Peter's confidence took a real battering last season. It was awful for the lad to go a whole season without a single goal to his name. The transfer fee of £5 million is a lot of money, so you should have big expectations as fans. But the pressure of living up to it was getting to Peter.

'We felt that if he was to improve here he needed to go away and get his confidence up somewhere else. By doing that, he can come back to Villa and do well.'

Crouch made his debut for Norwich on 13 September 2003, at home to Burnley – his fourth debut for different clubs and he was still only 22. But his new surroundings clearly had a positive effect as he opened the scoring for his new side just 58 minutes into his debut – his first goal in domestic football since scoring for Villa against Chelsea on the final day of the 2001–02 season.

The striker took full advantage of some slack play by Burnley defender Andy Todd as he tried to dribble out of defence, robbing the defender of possession before rolling the ball past goalkeeper Brian Jensen to kick off his career at Carrow Road in the perfect fashion and set Norwich on the way to a 2–0 win.

He was given a standing ovation when he was replaced in the 70th minute and was later named as man of the match. It was the ideal confidence booster for a player whose self-esteem must have been at an all-time low.

And, after just one match for the Canaries, he was already thinking about a future with them and away from Villa. He said, 'I won't rule out extending the loan until the end of the season – or something more. If all parties are happy, then I'm going to continue playing for Norwich. I need to play regularly and I just wasn't doing so at Villa.'

But while Crouch and his new boss Nigel Worthington were delighted, for Burnley manager Stan Ternent, the defeat, and particularly Crouch's performance, were a bitter pill to swallow. He revealed after his side's loss, 'I tried to sign Crouch before he went to Portsmouth – that's how highly I rate him.'

Those sentiments must have been music to Crouch's ears after such a long time in the doldrums, and he wasted no time in proving that his first goal in Norwich colours was no fluke by quickly adding a second to his tally just three days later, away to Gillingham.

Having scored his first senior goal for QPR against The Gills he had reason to approach the game in a confident mood, and that confidence was rewarded when he grabbed the winner in a 2–1 victory 25 minutes from time – Norwich's first away win of the season. The only downside was that he was booked for over-exuberance in celebrating his strike in front of the 1,000 travelling fans.

After just two games, it was obvious that Crouch had become a crowd favourite and the fans' support was much appreciated. He said, 'Scoring goals always helps a striker's confidence and it's great to hear fans singing my name again. I hope they won't suddenly forget the words!'

It was clear that the Villa misfit was an instant hit and he was obviously relishing life in a new environment, but there was one problem – the Norwich shorts!

The standard-issue pair were too short for Crouch, so several pairs were sent to a local tailors to have an extra four inches added. 'With my legs, I just feel more comfortable in long shorts,' said the big front man.

But, with that problem soon solved, Crouch netted his third goal for the club in his sixth game, a towering far-post header to earn them a 1–1 draw at West Ham, and then made it four in ten matches with Norwich's third in a convincing 3–1 win at Walsall as the Canaries continued their bright start to the season by cementing third place in the division.

His joy in that match, however, was tempered by his first sending-off in senior football after he was dismissed following an ugly confrontation with Saddlers' defender Paul Ritchie just a minute from the end of normal time.

That, though, was the solitary blot on his copybook during what turned out to be a hugely successful three months with Norwich. He played 14 games for the club, plus one other appearance as a substitute, scoring four goals, and by the time he left he had helped the club move from twelfth to second in the First Division table.

Norwich boss Nigel Worthington had hoped to extend the loan spell until the end of the season, but Villa were keen to have the new improved Crouch back among the fold. And, for his part, he was happy to return, determined to prove himself all over again.

'At my age, without doubt the best phase of my career should be just around the corner and I want it to be at

Villa,' he told reporters on his return to Villa Park. 'I have been very lucky with my career so far and had some great times at QPR and Pompey, but I felt when I signed for Villa that it was the perfect stage for me. The way it has gone so far I haven't had an extended run in the team, so I haven't really improved myself as a player since I've been there. That has meant Villa's supporters have not seen the best of me, but hopefully they will in the future.'

Crouch returned to the Villa first-team squad on 14 December 2003 for the derby game against Wolves. Although he did not get on the pitch, it did at least represent a return to the senior fold for the player who must have thought at one time that he no longer had a future at the club.

And three days later he was back in action at Villa Park – albeit only for the final seven minutes as a substitute – as the home side booked a place in the Carling Cup semi-finals with a 2–1 win over Chelsea.

He continued to be given only the odd few minutes here and there from the bench but, even so, it signalled a marked change of fortune; it was one he was happy to embrace as he looked to rebuild his career in the Midlands.

He admitted to the local Midlands media, 'Sometimes you have got to start wondering about your career at one club, especially when other people are doing well there and you are not. It can be frustrating watching two players up front, in the team all the time, and you want to get playing and can't.

'There is a major doubt about your future. That is why going to Norwich was such a help. I don't know if I really thought my Villa career was ever over. I always believed I had a future here. The good thing about Norwich was that we were winning and playing good football.

'I did not want to go to any old club. I had to choose carefully. They were disappointed when I left and I think Norwich wanted to keep me until the end of the season. I think I went down well with the fans there and they wanted me to stay, too.

'But there is another reason why I think I have a future at Villa. It is because David O'Leary called me back after the three-month loan spell ended. Obviously, that means I have some part to play with Villa, which suits me fine, because I want to prove myself at this club.

'Being at Norwich meant a good end to 2003; coming back to do well at Villa has made it a good start to 2004. Going away helped me. I thoroughly enjoyed my time at Norwich, just as coming back here has been good.

'I have played a part in a couple of games for Villa since, which is good. I'd like to play a bit more but, so far, the New Year has begun well. I was glad to see the back of the old year. It was one of those things where you are not getting a game, and going to Norwich was a chance to play football again.

'We did exceptionally well and I enjoyed my time there. It has given me a lot more confidence to do well at Villa, so, from that point of view, it has helped both parties. I always thought I could do a job at Villa if I was thrown in.

'I wouldn't say 2003 was a disaster, I just didn't have the chances to play that I would have liked. I went away, but I have come back and now I'd like to think that I will benefit from that. I am a stronger person, for sure, and certainly more confident. I have always believed in myself, never worried about whether I could make it. I have no qualms that I am going to do well here.

'I have spoken to the manager about my future and he has told me that I remain part of it here. He always wants me to be around the squad, which is encouraging.

'It makes it difficult that there are so many good strikers at Villa, but I have to be there if there is an injury or a drop in form. I will continue to work hard in training and will be waiting if there is a chance for me. Even being on the substitutes' bench is a compliment at this club. It is a boost for me that I can even make the bench. And there is always the chance that I might get on the pitch.

'I am only 22, I believe I have a big future here, and I feel good about it. I have been about, so it is easy to forget that I am young. I am hoping I have still got a long time left in me.'

That Crouch never gave up hope of resurrecting his Villa career is testimony to his enormous self-belief and only a truly cold-hearted Holte Ender would have begrudged him his first goal for the club since May 2002 when it finally arrived on 31 January 2004.

He scored Villa's second goal of the afternoon against Leicester at the Walkers Stadium and then, incredibly, followed it up with a second – and Villa's fifth – 22 minutes from time to complete a memorable occasion for both player and club.

It was a never-to-be-forgotten match for Crouch and provided the most perfect present, as just the day before he had celebrated his 23rd birthday. Afterwards, he revealed he had no recollection of the first goal; he had been knocked out by a defender's foot in the process of scoring it from Thomas Hitzlsperger's corner.

He told the *Birmingham Mail*, 'I didn't even know where I was to be honest, but, when I came round on the side of the pitch, I realised I'd scored and that was a great feeling. I wasn't dizzy for the second goal and I made sure I celebrated that one in front of the fans.

'They've been brilliant. I could sense that they were right behind me and it was superb. Those two goals are for those people who have stuck by me. Things have been difficult at times, but I'm now looking to take advantage of any opportunities that come my way.

'The lads have been brilliant and have been behind me 100 per cent, but this is just the start. There are a lot more years left in me, and I hope they'll all be at Aston Villa.

'I think I am turning the corner now. It was a great feeling to score the goals. I've got to make the most of this opportunity.'

But not everyone, it appeared, was quite so thrilled with Crouch's return to the Premiership goal-scoring list. Manager O'Leary, far from delivering a ringing endorsement of his struggling striker, chose instead to bemoan his lack of potency before the Leicester match.

He said after the match, 'If a striker is bought for £5 million then he is bought to score goals. I don't want to be told after a game that Crouch is playing really well. I want to know how many goals he's got. He got four in 15 games at Norwich in the First Division. I'm looking for a higher rate if he's going to help the cause at Villa.'

And just to emphasise the point that Crouch had a long way to go to convince the Irishman that he had a long-term future at the club, his reward for his two-goal salvo at Leicester was to be dumped back on the bench for the next game against Leeds as he made way for the fit-again Juan Pablo Angel.

And there he stayed until 10 April, when the Colombian was again ruled out of action by injury. Crouch's response? He scored Villa's first goal in a 2–2 draw against Bolton at the Reebok Stadium.

But still he could not avoid controversy of one kind or another, this time for a clash with Nicky Hunt that left Bolton boss Sam Allardyce fuming. He said, 'Crouch chopped Nicky down. If the referee had seen it, he should have given a red card.'

Crouch clearly saw the incident differently and, determined not to let it take the gloss off his goal-scoring return, he said, 'He [Hunt] is one of those players who tries to wind the opposition up. He gives a bit of banter, which is annoying, but I suppose I did bite. You can get sent off for that sort of thing in today's game, but he went down like he had been shot.'

It seemed that, no matter how hard people knocked him, Crouch simply would not go down. And this time he stayed in the team, at least for the next two matches, helping Villa to a 3–2 win over high-flying Chelsea and then a draw against Newcastle.

By the time Villa travelled to Middlesbrough on 24 April, however, Crouch was back on the bench. But again he would not be denied, replacing Angel with just 15 minutes remaining and earning Villa an absolutely crucial three points with a last-minute winner.

That victory lifted Villa to fifth place in the Premiership

with just three games remaining, meaning that Champions League football was tantalisingly within their reach – a remarkable turnaround in fortunes when you consider the woes of the club's previous campaign.

And Crouch, who at one stage during the season looked as though he would be shipped out to the First Division on a permanent basis, was daring to dream of the possibility of clashes against the likes of Real Madrid and AC Milan.

He told the local media, 'At the start of the season, we would have thought we were dreaming if you said we had a chance of Champions League football. I think we just wanted to improve from last year when we finished in the bottom half of the table. We were just looking to finish in the top half this season, but the way it has panned out we have a chance to get a massive prize at the end of it.

'To get in the top six, maybe even the top four, would be a massive bonus. That is there for us now and hopefully we can see it out.'

Crouch had played no small part in Villa's surge up the table since his return from Norwich and he admitted that, perhaps for the first time, he felt as though he belonged at the club.

'I'm feeling great at the minute and it's superb to be a part of Villa,' he added. 'It has been going well for me recently and the team have been doing well too. Hopefully, I have proved that, when thrown in, I can do a job. We have had a couple of injuries recently and I have been getting a run out which has been good for me.

'We have been winning too, and I feel I have been doing reasonably well. Playing with confidence is the key and, at the minute, I am playing with as much of it [confidence] as anyone. The team seems to be more confident this season; we believe we can win whether we are home or away.

'Last year, we were a little more negative. We went away and we often thought it would be a miracle if we could get something. Now we are going away from home believing we can get a result at any away ground and I think that adds a lot more to everyone's game.

'We raise it a little more and are not afraid to make mistakes. I think you need to be playing with confidence to perform well. If you are scared of having a shot or making a pass, then it hinders your game.

'Every player wants to be a part of the Champions League; it is the biggest club trophy you can be involved in. If we get there it would be a really great season for me and the club. And it will have been a really pleasing season for the fans, because they have had a lot to put up with over the last few years.'

Ultimately, however, Villa's challenge for the Champions League failed, as they could only draw their penultimate game at Southampton, leaving them in fifth place and with a UEFA Cup spot to play for in their final game of the season at home to Manchester United.

Not that O'Leary believed failing to finish in the top four was a failure. Indeed, he claimed finishing sixth – outside of the European places – would still represent a fantastic achievement.

Ahead of the United game he insisted, 'I came here because I had to shut a few people up,' referring to his sacking at Leeds. 'The next step is hopefully to get some new players in the summer, free transfers and loan players. We have a limited amount of money and, with the amount of players we need to bring in here, I will be looking for some bargains.

'I don't think it's any coincidence that the top five clubs spend the most money. They're the ones with the biggest crowds, the biggest squads and the ones who will be in the top five for years to come.

'Arsenal will be there for quite a long time, United too, and Mr Abramovich [at Chelsea] will be there for quite a long time as well. Liverpool and Newcastle also have enormous spending power. That is set in stone.

'Can we finish best of the rest? I can't say what the fans might feel, but if people think we can finish fifth or fourth next season that would mean finishing higher than Liverpool and Newcastle and I find that hard to believe.

'If we can keep challenging for a European place, that represents success for us. We finished 16th last year and just avoided relegation, so we have certainly improved on that.

'Finishing sixth has no European place, but it would be a fantastic prize for us.'

O'Leary may have been saying that publicly, but privately he was surely focusing on finishing fifth and ensuring European football. Whether he was trying to take the pressure off his players ahead of the United game or not, it didn't work. They lost 2–0 at Villa Park to drop to sixth, despite United having both Darren Fletcher and Cristiano Ronaldo sent off – and lost out on that European place to Newcastle on goal difference.

For all O'Leary's talk of sixth place being a 'fantastic prize', you can be sure it was a sentiment the players and fans did not share. In truth, it had been a nightmare finale to a season that had promised so much for Villa, but at least they could take consolation from having shown a vast improvement on their final position of 16th the previous year.

As for Crouch, he could take heart from the fact that he had scored four goals in 17 games, the vast majority of them as a substitute, since his return from Norwich. And he did at least have the honour of picking up a First Division winners' medal, courtesy of the games he played for the Canaries and their subsequent title success.

So, at least he had something to smile about as he ended his first full season at Villa, albeit one that had been interrupted by a three-month stint at Norwich. Little did he realise at the time, however, that it was also to be his last.

CHAPTER 4

FROM VILLAIN TO SAINT

Footballers often talk about the need to feel settled in their environment before they can produce their best. It's one reason that is often cited when a club's new signing struggles to hit form straight away: that the player is likely to bemoan the fact that he is living in a hotel, especially if his family has not yet made the move with him.

Until they are firmly ensconced in a new home, surrounded by their own home comforts, they often find it difficult to concentrate fully on what they are being paid to do – deliver the goods on the pitch.

As he closed the book on season 2003–04 – only his fourth in league football, remember – Crouch could reflect on the fact that he had already moved three times, four if you count his time in Norfolk with Norwich.

He had been forced to leave London, where he had grown up and where his family lived, as a 19-year-old, when QPR sold him to Portsmouth. But, within 12 months, he was swapping the south coast for the Midlands, and the blue of Pompey for the claret and blue of Aston Villa. Little wonder, then, that his time at Villa Park had not gone as well he would have hoped.

He never used his geographical upheaval as an excuse for his lack of goals, however, and remained determined to establish himself at Villa and prove that he could be a long-term success for them and that the £5 million the Midlands club had paid to Portsmouth was, in fact, money well spent.

By now, however, it had become apparent that he was not O'Leary's idea of the ideal centre-forward, and, when Southampton approached the Irishman with a £2 million offer for his misfiring hitman, he was only too happy to accept.

So Crouch, amazingly, was going back to the south coast – his fifth club in just four years, not including Norwich.

O'Leary's decision to sell Crouch – for a loss of £3 million in just two years, don't forget – was greeted with enthusiasm by some, but with puzzlement by others, among them the former Villa boss Graham Taylor, who had signed Crouch for the club.

He later reflected in the *Birmingham Mail*, 'I thought that because O'Leary had watched at close quarters how Niall Quinn had turned from a gangly 18-year-old into an international centre-forward of some repute that Peter would be all right. But we all have our ideas on players and he sold him, which left Peter at a crossroads.'

Crouch, for his part, took the move in his giant stride;

in the same way he had seemed to approach both success and failure during his career so far. As far as he was concerned, if one manager did not want him, he would simply pack his bags and go off and play for one that did.

On his arrival at his new club he told reporters, 'Southampton manager Paul Sturrock and chairman Rupert Lowe are extremely ambitious for the club and I was very impressed with what they had to say. I had a few options open to me at the end of last season, but I always thought I would stay at Villa. However, once they accepted offers for me and I had spoken to Southampton, I knew I wanted to join.

'While I don't think the Villa fans always saw the best of me, I don't think I was given the opportunities I deserved. But I am fit and raring to go now.'

The only hint of trepidation about the move regarded the way the Saints' fans would receive him. He had, after all, committed the cardinal sin of having previously played for their arch-rivals Portsmouth.

He hoped the fans would 'forgive' him for that and added, 'I am a Saints player now and the club will get all my commitment.'

Sturrock, who was beginning his first full season as Southampton manager, having taken over the reins the previous March, also seemed happy with his recruitment of the 23-year-old former England Under-21 international.

And he rejected suggestions that the new arrival would mean his side reverting to a 'Wimbledon-style' game plan of hitting long balls towards Crouch and James Beattie.

'It simply means we have more options in attack now Peter has joined us,' he said at the time of Crouch's signing. 'He will be very good cover for James [Beattie] and can play alongside him if it comes to us having to chase a game.

'Peter can also do well alongside Kevin Phillips, or if we identify a certain weakness in the opposition. We also have Brett Ormerod and now I have plenty of choices up front, which can only be good for the team.'

However, although Sturrock spoke in glowing terms about his new signing, doubts appeared to surface following a pre-season friendly against Swindon. Although the Saints won the match 2–1, the manager was not entirely thrilled with the tactics employed by his side.

And, during the game, he took the unprecedented step of banning his players from 'just lashing balls' up front to Crouch. He said in his post-match press conference, 'The problem is that, when you have a really big man up front, players revert to type and we finished up in the first half just lashing balls up to the boy Crouch.

'And to be fair I don't want them playing it in the air because he's reasonably poor in the air for his height. It finished up that we couldn't get service, couldn't keep the ball up the front, the midfield were dropping back to receive the pass so there was no support to the front players – so we were very disjointed.

'It's not anybody's intention at this football club to play a long-ball scenario, but it is easy to do that. I told them at half-time that in the second half they weren't allowed to play that ball at all and it worked.'

Sturrock, though, was clearly concerned that in the heat

of battle his players would forget his instructions and would be unable to resist the temptation to 'go long' towards Crouch. He was left out of the starting line-up for the club's final warm-up fixture a week later, a 3–1 win over Italian side Chievo Verona, and, when the season kicked off a week later, Crouch found himself in a familiar role – on the bench.

And, in a further twist of irony, he found himself back on the bench at Villa Park. The fixture computer had, remarkably, handed his new club a visit to his old one on the first day of the season.

But Crouch was denied a proper chance to show the Villa fans what they were missing, being given only the final 22 minutes of the match as a replacement for Ormerod, by which time Southampton were trailing by two goals to nil. There was one boost for him, however, as he was given a warm reception by both sets of supporters.

He told the Southampton website after his first match in Saints' colours, 'It was a great reception coming back [to Villa Park] and it is nice when the fans recognise your efforts. It was a lovely feeling. And it was nice to get a warm reception from the Southampton fans, too, because I need that. I hope I can repay them in my displays.

'Unfortunately, we did not do it for them in this game, which was very disappointing. It was the first game of the season and there is a long way still to go, so we have to put this behind us and move on. We have to look at what we did well and build on it.'

Crouch was also forced to sit out Southampton's first home game of the season, a 3–2 win over Blackburn, when he had to content himself with a role as a non-playing substitute. No one at the game that evening, though, could have an inkling of the drama that was about to unfold, with manager Sturrock set to be sacked by the club after just 13 games in charge, just a couple of days after having received the public backing of chairman Rupert Lowe.

The decision by Lowe to replace Sturrock was to have repercussions for the whole club, and most certainly for Crouch. In the early stages following the Scot's departure, however, which Lowe attributed partly to pressures from the media, there was simply bitterness and resentment among supporters who were furious at their chairman's actions.

Nick Illingsworth, the chairman of Southampton Independent Supporters' Association, said, 'Arsenal can go 42 games without losing. We can't even go 42 with the same manager. They keep leaving and Rupert Lowe is the common denominator. I am sure he is in for a lot of stick, because fans have become very disgruntled with his behaviour.

'He had their respect for taking the club from The Dell to St Mary's and for reaching the FA Cup final. Now he has lost that respect and will have to work hard to get it back.'

And former manager Lawrie McMenemy also attacked the decision to dispense with Sturrock just two games into the season. He said in an interview in the *Sun*, 'Southampton are known for their consistency throughout football. That is why we had an element of success. We were never as big as Arsenal or Manchester

United, but we were able to get on and manage. On Saturday, Lowe was praising himself for success by saying, "We are not the club we were." Damn right we're not; we've had six managers in six years. We've become a laughing stock.

'We've had big names and experienced people, but why do the likes of Glenn Hoddle, Gordon Strachan and Graeme Souness walk away from the club? The club has got to look at itself. And to try and blame the media for getting rid of this lad [Sturrock] is disgraceful.'

It was a desperate start to the new season for the club. For Crouch, it represented a nightmare beginning to his career at Saints. Just when he would have wanted a quiet settling-in period to allow him to build up his confidence again, he found himself in the middle of a club in turmoil.

And it soon became clear that there was going to be no short-term fix. Assistant manager Steve Wigley was given control of the first team and his first game came at home to Bolton, just 48 hours after Sturrock's dismissal.

And Bolton boss Sam Allardyce stoked the fires on the eve of that encounter, adding his voice to those who had condemned Sturrock's sacking. He told reporters in his pre-match press conference, 'The pressure on managers now is unbelievable and it seems owners are not prepared to give anybody a real crack of the whip to try to prove themselves. Managers are always the scapegoats and I think Paul has lost his job on that basis.'

The atmosphere that night at St Mary's was hostile to say the least, with Lowe subjected to the fans' fury. Chants of 'sack the board' and 'we want Rupert out' rang around the ground that night; it hardly helped the cause of the Southampton players.

And it appeared they were as shell-shocked as the fans by the events of the previous couple of days as they found themselves 2–0 down after less than half an hour and on the brink of a second defeat in three games.

Crouch was once again named among the substitutes, and once again he was given a little over 20 minutes to influence events, going on as a 69th-minute replacement for Rory Delap. And, while there was to be no joy for the team as a whole, there was at least a crumb of comfort for Crouch as he netted his first goal in a Southampton shirt.

It would be fair to say it was not a classic, more a case of him bundling the ball over the line from Paul Telfer's right-wing cross but, as any striker at any level of the game will tell you, it's crucial to get off the mark early for a new team.

It was a difficult atmosphere in which to take charge of the side for the first time, but Wigley was not prepared to offer that up as a reason for the defeat. He told the assembled media afterwards, 'There are no excuses. We know what our jobs are from one to eleven. We have got good players and we should have played better than we did.

'The crowd played their part in trying to get us back in the game and we nearly stole a point at the end, which we would not have deserved, but because they stayed with us that at least gave us a chance.

'There were some boos at the end, but the supporters have every right to show their feelings. They pay their money and they work very hard to earn it and they deserved better than they got today.

'Those boos did not hurt as much as the performance. The boos I can accept. The performance I cannot.'

Crouch's goal, though, was not enough to earn him a place in the starting XI for the next match at Chelsea and it was not until a Carling Cup tie at Northampton, on 22 September 2004, that he made his first start in a Saints shirt.

That looked a tricky tie for a side that had won just once in their first six games of the season, but Southampton came through comfortably enough in a 3–0 victory. But it was an entirely different story in the Premiership.

They lost two and drew four of their next six league matches, meaning that they had won just one Premiership match by the first week of November. But there was far worse to come.

Southampton travelled to Championship side Watford on 9 November for a Carling Cup fourth-round tie and a chance to get their season back on track. The night turned into a horror show, however, as they were humbled 5–2 and dumped out of the competition. For Crouch, while he would have clearly relished the opportunity to try to help his side, there must have been a tinge of relief that he was confined to the safety of the subs' bench.

It was a disastrous result and led to widespread speculation that Wigley would soon be joining Sturrock on the list of Southampton's former managers, with the bookies refusing to take any more bets on him being the next Premiership boss to be sacked. In his press conference after the game, he admitted, 'I'll take a long look at myself after this performance. Who knows how I will be feeling in a day or so. I didn't think we had a performance like that in us. I was obviously wrong.'

Meanwhile, former players and managers were queuing up to have their say and pour scorn on the current regime at the club. Ex-boss Dave Merrington told the *Sun*, 'If the chairman's going to sack Wigley, he has to look at himself, because the number of managers that they have had now has made them a laughing stock.

'He would probably say, "Well, I've only ever sacked one manager," but you have to question why managers have come and gone so quickly. There's complete instability in the club. I think if this was an industry outside of football, then the chairman of the company would be in question.'

Peter Osgood, however, a former crowd favourite at The Dell, laid the blame squarely at Wigley's door. He told the same newspaper, 'Rupert Lowe has run the club brilliantly until now. He had a good manager in Gordon Strachan and had moved into a new stadium at St Mary's.

'The team finished eighth in the Premiership, reached the FA Cup final and got into Europe. But then the manager went and the chairman wanted to appoint Glenn Hoddle as his replacement.

'But the fans were against it and so Steve Wigley was given the job instead. He was the fans' choice and the players'. But Steve has not won a single Premiership game so far. He knows that it is results that count at the end of the day and he hasn't got them.

'He's done his best, but, if his best is not good enough, then he is not the man for the job. The chairman must get it right this time and I think it is time to appoint a proven manager with good experience who has done it all.'

The situation provided an extraordinary backdrop to the build-up to what was without doubt the biggest game of the season so far – the derby against hated local rivals Portsmouth. And it was widely assumed that anything other than victory at St Mary's would signal an end to Wigley's reign.

As it was, goals from Dexter Blackstock and Kevin Phillips – Crouch was again a non-playing substitute – ensured Southampton recovered from the shock of going behind to an Andreas Jakobsson own goal after just 12 minutes to earn Wigley his first win in 11 attempts. It also provided him with a stay of execution.

And it was a far happier manager who faced the press after the game. He said, 'I am relieved and pleased. The midweek result put pressure on us, but it created the right atmosphere for today. I threw the players into a room together on Wednesday and told them we needed some home truths.

'The Watford game was the lowest point in my career, but it's been quickly followed by a high in beating Portsmouth. I've hardly been able to sleep since that Watford match, and if I'm honest I knew the Portsmouth game was a must-win for me. But I have the players behind me and believe I have the club behind me, too.

'We have now gone four matches in the Premier League without defeat and if we can keep this going we can shoot up the table. I have spoken to the chairman a couple of times this week and he has been very supportive. I believe I will still be here at the end of the season.

'I'm sick of talking about my position, and after today I won't be doing it any more.'

That may have been his stance, but it soon became apparent that, whatever he may have said or thought, the speculation surrounding his future was not going to go away. And after three further matches – away defeats to Norwich and Manchester United, and a home draw with Crystal Palace – the inevitable occurred. Wigley was sacked.

And, in another sensational twist, his replacement was announced almost immediately as Harry Redknapp, who had acrimoniously parted company with fierce local rivals Portsmouth just a couple of weeks before.

But, far from venting his spleen against Lowe and engaging in a bitter war of words with his former boss about the speed with which we had been replaced, Wigley, while obviously disappointed not to have made a success of things in the first-team hot-seat, stressed that he was thankful to have been given the chance in the first place.

He told the *Daily Mail*, 'I don't regret taking the job at all. It was a great opportunity for me and I wouldn't have missed it for the world. People might wonder whether it came a bit too soon for me, but you don't think about things like that.

'What you actually think when a Premiership chairman offers you the job of manager is, "There are only 20 of these up for grabs." Now what could my answer possibly be?

'Now it has been taken away, I can honestly say there

are no regrets. My only regret would have been if I had turned it down. I knew that management was results-driven and that if we were struggling I would be in trouble.

'Just before I left, I think our run was one defeat in five or six games. We were getting somewhere, but I was beginning to hear signals that time was running out for me. I needed a result quickly, but what did the fixture list throw up? Manchester United at Old Trafford.

'You've got it all to do there at the best of times and it began to look as if the odds were stacked against me. But I've never ducked a challenge in my life and I kept at it, working with the first-team players and keeping an eye on the kids coming through. In fact, that's how it all ended. It's ironic, after all I did to get the Academy off the ground, that I was told I was out of a job a few minutes after our youth team's game at QPR last Tuesday.

'The chairman took me to one side and said, "Look, I'm sorry about this. There have been a few wobbles on the board and I have to admit I also feel that perhaps it's time for a change."

'He then told me Harry Redknapp had been offered the job. Now that might have riled some people, but I'm not going to whinge about my job being offered to someone else before I'd been told about it. That happens in football.

'I appreciated the chairman doing his best to keep me at the club in another capacity. He really did try, but I just said, "Thanks for letting me manage the team, but I think it's best we make a clean break."

'He told me to sleep on it, but I knew my answer would be the same the next day. It wasn't bitterness. It was just that the new manager would want his own people with him and it seemed the right moment to start a new chapter in my life.

'I know some people will be looking for me to slaughter the chairman. But I won't. We had a great working relationship and my only regret is that I wasn't able to lift them out of the bottom three.

'I happen to think Harry is a good appointment. He has so much life and vitality and he will breathe that into the club. I hope they stay up and I think they will.'

Wigley's departure and the arrival of Redknapp, while obviously a further upheaval for all concerned at the club, did offer everyone the chance to start with a clean slate. None more so than Crouch.

His first few months at the club had been anything but happy. He had had problems with a knee injury but, even when fit, he had been unable to command a place in the side and it became increasingly clear that Wigley did not rate him.

'It was probably a bit difficult for him when he first arrived at the club,' first-team coach Dennis Rofe later admitted in the press. 'Paul Sturrock had bought him and he lasted two games of that season. When a manager leaves after two games, you feel a bit uncertain, particularly as we had James Beattie and Kevin Phillips. Peter probably wondered if he'd made the right move or the wrong move.'

And Crouch could have been forgiven for viewing the appointment of Redknapp with some trepidation. After all, one of his first moves as Portsmouth boss had been to sanction the striker's move to Aston Villa.

Redknapp, though, was quick to reassure Crouch that he had a future at St Mary's. Crouch later recalled in an interview on the club's website, 'Having been sold by him I did wonder if he rated me, but the manager told me that he didn't sell me from Pompey because he didn't fancy me, but because another club was prepared to pay a lot of money. And he used that money to turn them into a totally different team and establish them in the Premiership.'

In fact, in an immediate show of faith, Redknapp named Crouch in his first line-up to face Middlesbrough at St Mary's just three days after his appointment as manager. And the big striker did not let his new boss down.

On what looked like being a glorious day for all concerned, Crouch scored Southampton's second goal midway through the second half to earn them a 2–0 lead, following Kevin Phillips's opener on the stroke of half-time. But, just as it appeared that there was to be a fairytale beginning to Redknapp's reign, disaster struck.

Firstly, with just a minute remaining, Danny Higginbotham deflected a corner into his own net and then, with just seconds left on the clock and with Saints desperately clinging on for a vital victory, Boro winger Stewart Downing delivered a devastating blow with a perfect left-foot shot to rescue a point for the visitors.

Redknapp admitted to journalists after the match, 'After our second goal, I was looking for the end. With a minute to go, we're just looking to defend a corner, it skims off one of our players and, suddenly, the tension creeps in. It's been difficult picking a team; we had a practice on Thursday. I chopped and changed it but, apart from the very end, I was happy with what went on.'

What that game did prove, however, was that Southampton looked to have the battling qualities to mount a challenge for survival, and that it had been folly on Wigley's part to ignore the merits of Crouch and consign him to the reserves for such long periods of time.

Crouch, naturally, retained his place in the side for the next game – a return to his first professional club, Tottenham. It did not, though, go as he would have wished, with Southampton finding themselves on the wrong end of a 5–1 scoreline. The one consolation was that he found the target once again.

On the negative side, results did not take the immediate upward turn that the club's hierarchy or supporters were hoping for. The next three games yielded just two points, courtesy of home draws against Charlton and Fulham, either side of a defeat away to Manchester City.

It meant that, as Redknapp approached his seventh game in charge of the club, a nasty-looking FA Cup third-round tie away at Northampton, he was still searching for his first victory. And he would need to achieve it without striker James Beattie, who was sold to Everton in a £6 million deal three days before the trip to the Sixfields Stadium.

It was, of course, Southampton's second visit to Northampton that season. Their first, in the Carling Cup back in September, had resulted in Wigley's first victory in charge. And so there was a neat symmetry in the fact their second trip should earn Redknapp his inaugural success.

The scoreline on this occasion was 3–1, with Crouch netting the second goal four minutes before half-time.

It was a much-needed boost for the whole club, particularly as it came so soon after Beattie's departure for Goodison Park.

And Crouch was determined that he would be the man to replace Beattie in the Southampton fans' affections and to score the goals to keep them in the Premiership. He said in an interview with the club's website, 'I was a bit concerned when I first arrived here and I was not getting in the team, or even on the subs' bench. But deep down I always thought that Beattie would be sold in the transfer window, and that was when I would get a chance.

'So, when I heard he was on his way to Everton, I was happily out there in the car park waving him goodbye! James was superb here, and we are good pals, but now it's up to me to cement my place and prove that his replacement is already here. Hopefully, I can be as successful as he was.'

Crouch scored again in the next game, a narrow 2–1 defeat at Newcastle, before two games in a week that ensured not only that the Saints supporters were no longer talking about the departure of Beattie, but that also went a long way towards shaping the striker's future career.

Firstly came Redknapp's first three Premiership points since his appointment at St Mary's. And what a scalp to earn them against, coming as they did against none other than Liverpool. Once more, Crouch was on the scoresheet, grabbing his side's second goal after 22 minutes, having set up the first for David Prutton with only five minutes on the clock. That made the scoreline 2–0 and that was how the game finished.

Redknapp, naturally enough, was ecstatic. He said in his post-match press conference, 'It was an excellent win, a terrific performance. It feels fantastic to have got my first league win here. There is still a long way to go and we have a lot of tough fixtures, but this is just what we needed. If we keep playing like that, we have a big chance of staying up.'

The Southampton boss also had words of praise for Crouch, who had to shoulder the attacking responsibilities as a lone striker with Kevin Phillips absent through injury. Redknapp added, 'Peter Crouch did a great job up front on his own where he held the ball up well.'

Crouch, too, was thrilled, and hailed the victory as Southampton's best performance of the season. He told the club's website, 'It is a massive lift. Beating somebody like Liverpool at home is always good for the spirits and the dressing room was buzzing afterwards, but we have got to go on from here.

'Once you get that one win, sometimes that can build the confidence and you go on a little run, that is something that we really need now. We need to put some wins together, so hopefully this can be the start of that.'

And if the players needed any inspiration to embark on the kind of winning run they would need to achieve Premiership safety, they only needed to look a week ahead towards their next game – an FA Cup fourth-round tie at home to Portsmouth.

Games don't come any bigger on the south coast than the derby clash between those two sides and, for Crouch, there was added significance attached to the game, given his previous allegiance to Portsmouth.

That, though, paled into insignificance when compared to the Portsmouth fans' feelings towards Redknapp, the man who had done so much to establish them as a Premiership force but who had then committed the mortal sin of joining the enemy. As if it were needed, that merely added extra spice to what was already an eagerly anticipated grudge match.

And it was one that Crouch was looking forward to. He hoped the visiting fans would recognise the part he – and indeed Redknapp – had played in getting Portsmouth into the position they were currently in.

'Looking at the decision Harry made to sell me from Portsmouth, it was obviously the right one because he used the money wisely and made them the club they are now,' Crouch told the Southampton website. 'When I left it was obvious that we were struggling and it looked like we were relegation candidates in the First Division. So for him to go in there and establish them as a Premiership team was something else really.

'Because of that I am surprised by the amount of hate he has received [since moving to Southampton]. It has been a bit strange if you ask me, but that is football, I suppose, and, with the rivalry being so great, it is one of those things.'

Crouch, though, admitted before the game that he wasn't sure how he would react if he were to score against his old club. He went on to say, 'If I do score, I couldn't tell you what my celebration would be. It is a heat-of-the-moment thing and I suppose it sort of depends on the reaction I get from them [the Portsmouth fans] as well. But that is certainly not something that would bother me.

'I don't think I owe them anything. I had a great year there, scored goals and they paid £1.5 million for me and then sold me for £5 million within one season. Harry built what they are now with that money.

'I did nothing wrong while I was there, but I have crossed over that line I suppose. The rivalry is a big thing to the fans, but hopefully I won't get too bad a reception – certainly not as bad as some people's!'

As it turned out, Redknapp – and Crouch in particular – certainly gave the Pompey fans something to jeer about in an extraordinary finale that a scriptwriter for *Roy of the Rovers* would have struggled to surpass.

With just a minute left on the clock and with the two sides heading for a replay at Fratton Park, level as they were with the scores at 1–1, referee Steve Bennett awarded a controversial penalty as Prutton's cross was blocked by Matthew Taylor's arm.

As the crowd on all four sides of the ground went mad – for differing reasons, of course – Crouch calmly picked up the ball and placed it on the penalty spot. At that moment, Redknapp's heart sank.

He admitted after the match, 'We never thought about getting a penalty, so when we got one I wondered who was going to take it. Crouchy grabbed the ball and, being truthful, I never saw him as a penalty taker. I didn't know what he was going to do – I thought he might head it! I would be a liar if I said I felt confident he would score it.

'I said, "I'm not sure I fancy him to get this," and someone next to me said he would do it – so I thought, "That's OK then." And it was! Jim Smith was even worse than me. He said he couldn't score it, but Peter kept his nerve and slotted it in nicely.

'If someone is confident enough to take it, then fine by me. In those circumstances, you have to have someone who fancies it. Fair play to him because it took some nerve at that stage of a local derby, and against his old club. He did well.'

But, while Redknapp and his assistant Smith may have had their doubts, Crouch insisted afterwards that he was never worried. He revealed that he had received an extra boost after beating penalty king Matt Le Tissier in a specially staged shoot-out for Sky TV in the build-up to the game.

He told the media at St Mary's, 'Maybe a few people around the ground were surprised when I stepped up, but I was always going to take it. Dennis Rofe had asked me beforehand if I was OK to be on penalties and I was more than happy.

'I was feeling quite confident because I'd had a fun contest with Matt. We had a few practice goes, which I stuck away, and then I got ten out of ten [Le Tissier missed two], so I fancied my chances. It was a big moment and it took a while for the kick to be taken, but I was delighted to see it go in.'

It confirmed that hero status would be bestowed upon Crouch by Saints fans and it marked a sharp upturn in confidence since the troubled days under Wigley, days when he was largely ignored and left to toil in the reserves.

First-team coach Kevin Bond later admitted, 'The biggest thing was having someone put their confidence in him. He always had confidence in himself but, when Harry came, that was without doubt the turning point. All Harry did was put him in the side, said he would stay in and told him what a good player he was.

'Southampton were struggling like mad at the wrong end of the table; there were injuries to Kevin Phillips and James Beattie and all the while Crouch was doing nothing, kicking his heels in the reserves. Harry put him in and he produced the goods straight away, gave us the goals and the all-round play. He has a terrific touch, he brings people into the game and he has terrific awareness. We were scratching our heads as to how other people hadn't used him sooner.'

But, while FA Cup success was providing a welcome distraction from the Premiership relegation fight, top-flight survival remained the club's top priority, and with games beginning to run out it was vital that the Saints started picking up points sooner rather than later.

They were brought back down to earth with a bump following their cup success over Pompey when they were beaten 2–1 at Birmingham in their next fixture, before a typical quirk of fate – one that often seems to occur in football – saw that the next visitors to St Mary's were Everton – complete with James Beattie in tow. It was to be another heart-stopping clash.

Before the game, Crouch paid tribute to the part Redknapp had played in giving him the confidence to fill Beattie's boots. 'You have just got to try and impress whoever you play under and fortunately for me the gaffer has been brilliant, has shown a lot of faith in me and given me my chance,' he told the club's website.

Peter Crouch was signed to Tottenham Hotspur at 17 but, despite his early promise, he failed to make the grade at White Hart Lane.

A reserve match between Spurs and West Ham United. Crouch is confronted and then floored by West Ham's Chris Coyne.

Above: Crouch was nicknamed 'Rodders' because of his similarity to the *Only Fools and Horses* character.

Below left: At Loftus Road, Crouch's talent began to shine through. Here, he is challenged by Steve Yates during a Division One match between QPR and Tranmere Rovers.

Below right: The height stuff. Crouch towers over Gavin McCann of Aston Villa.

Above: Crouch bangs one in the net for Southampton against Liverpool in 2005.

Below: The Saints go marching in. Southampton manager Harry Redknapp gestures to Crouch from the sidelines.

Celebrating a goal against Northampton in the FA Cup third round in January 2005.

Having a laugh with Jamie Redknapp.

Above: Peter Crouch scores the winner in the FA Cup fourth round against Portsmouth and, *below left*, celebrates with his team-mates.

Below right: Crouch demonstrates the height advantage.

Crystal Palace v. Southampton, May 2005.

Above left: Crouch puts his long legs to good use.

Above right: Acknowledging the crowd.

Below left: Not so happy now – Crouch is shown the red card and, *below right*, the Palace fans jeer as he disappears down the players' tunnel.

He added, 'I've had a few managers already throughout my career and it can be frustrating, because at one time you can be a favourite and then somebody else comes in and you are totally disregarded.

'I am 23 now and I feel like I am about 30 because I have moved around so much, so I would like to settle down here. I really do want to stay here for as long as possible, first and foremost to keep the club in the Premiership, and then push on from there next season.'

One man who was not surprised to see Crouch doing so well was his former boss at Tottenham and QPR, Gerry Francis. He told the *Evening Standard*, 'Harry has devised a system of play to get the best out of Peter. He looks the player we knew he could be.'

The match against Everton, however, could have changed Redknapp's opinion for the worse. Things started badly for Southampton when Beattie – who else? – opened the scoring after just four minutes on his return to St Mary's, but by half-time the scores were level courtesy of Crouch's fifth goal in six games.

And, when Henri Camara fired the Saints into the lead ten minutes after the interval, it looked as though they were on their way to three more precious points. Then came ten fateful seconds at the end of the game that no Southampton fan will ever forget.

The ball broke to Crouch and he sprinted away towards goal. He could have headed for the corner flag and opted to see out the duration of the match with a spot of time-wasting but, like all good strikers, his instincts took over and he fired in his shot.

However, his effort lacked power and, as his team-mates berated him for gifting Everton possession, goalkeeper Nigel Martyn launched the ball downfield and substitute Marcus Bent pounced to smash home an equaliser that Everton scarcely deserved.

History had cruelly repeated itself after the Middlesbrough game and the look on the face of the Saints boss when referee Andy D'Urso below the final whistle was enough to evoke sympathy in even the most hard-hearted of opposition fans. After all, at one time or another, every football supporter has had that same nauseous feeling of seeing their side denied their just rewards.

After the game Redknapp said, 'I would never criticise a striker for trying to score a goal. He had made a fantastic break and was one-on-one with the goalkeeper. In that situation any decent forward is convinced he will score and his whole instinct tells him to go for goal.

'How would it have looked if he had got inside the penalty box and then headed for the corner flag? Ridiculous. Mind you, if I'm honest, I'd much rather he had smashed his shot somewhere into Row Z, so we could have got our defensive shape again and collected the three points!'

It was becoming clear that the concession of late goals and too many draws were combining to threaten Southampton's Premiership status. Dropping another two points against Everton left the club second from bottom in the table, and cost them the chance of closing the gap on Crystal Palace – who were in 17th, the final survival spot – to just a single point.

And their inability to convert one point into three would cost them in their next two league matches as well – an away stalemate against fellow strugglers West Bromwich Albion and a home draw against high-flying Arsenal.

Crouch was once more on target against the Gunners, scoring the Saints' goal in the 1–1 draw at St Mary's to cancel out Freddie Ljungberg's opener. On most days, a point against one of the Premiership's established top four – particularly having played with ten men for the whole of the second half after David Prutton's sending-off – would have been hailed as a terrific result. But in Southampton's current plight, only wins were good enough.

Although those two draws had seen them overtake Norwich and move up to third from bottom, they had lost ground on Palace and now trailed them by four points. And the gap to Blackburn, who were one place above the Londoners in 16th place, was now up to seven points, with just ten games remaining.

And, to make matters worse, Prutton, unsurprisingly, received a lengthy ban – ten games – for his crazy behaviour against Arsenal. Having been sent off for a dreadful challenge on Robert Pires, the midfielder then grabbed hold of referee Wiley and appeared to make verbal threats to one of his assistant referees.

Redknapp was forced on to the pitch to intervene, and he said after the match, 'Prutton will have to learn that he is doing us no favours with challenges like that.'

The player himself, after learning that he had been charged with misconduct by the Football Association, was full of remorse. He told the *Evening Standard*, 'I haven't got a leg to stand on. I've looked at it, I've thought about it and I've read about it. It's an horrendous situation which I've never found myself in before and, hopefully, never will again. I need to apologise, firstly to the ref, and to [Robert] Pires. I thought he had made a meal of it but, with hindsight, I've seen the pictures and heard about what happened to his leg, so I'm incredibly sorry about that. I would never go on to the pitch to try and hurt anyone.

'To be honest, I can't remember before and afterwards. It's a bit of a blur. But I felt I'd let my friends down, my team-mates, the management and everyone in the ground because it was just ludicrous.'

For Redknapp, it merely rubbed salt into the wounds. Time was running out if Southampton were to mount an unlikely escape act. They showed again that they had the spirit for the fight in their next two matches, a 3–1 FA Cup fifth-round replay win over Brentford, including two more goals for Crouch, and a vital 1–0 home success over Tottenham in the Premiership.

After that win over his former club, Jamie Redknapp paid tribute to Crouch. 'I cannot speak highly enough of him because he has done brilliantly for us this season,' he told the club's website. 'I don't think at the moment, in this country, there are many forwards in the sort of form that he is. If somebody told me that he was in the next England squad, that wouldn't surprise me.

'He is such a weapon and, if you use him right, he can cause anyone problems. There were times against Spurs when Ledley King and Anthony Gardner just couldn't deal with him, and they are two excellent defenders. He has been immense this season.'

However, despite those three points against the men

from White Hart Lane, Southampton still remained in the bottom three. Now there were just nine games left.

Before the toil for league points continued, however, there was the small matter of an FA Cup quarter-final against Manchester United on the horizon. As you would expect, a sell-out crowd of almost 31,000 packed into St Mary's for the occasion, but the match started badly when Roy Keane gave the visitors the lead after only two minutes ... and it got progressively worse.

Cristiano Ronaldo added a second on the stroke of half-time, before a Paul Scholes double in the second half completed the misery for the home side. They had suffered their heaviest ever defeat at the stadium and it was also Redknapp's first defeat at the ground.

It was a chastening loss and one that signalled an end to the club's six-match unbeaten run but, in the grand scheme of things, it wasn't too damaging. Of course, everyone at the club would have loved a return to Cardiff for the FA Cup final, where they had lost to Arsenal in 2003, but they also recognised that the clamour for Premiership points remained the focus.

They needed to get the United defeat out of their system as soon as possible, and they did so in fine style in their very next game. Crouch led the way again with two more goals, the second of which was an absolutely sublime side-foot volley, as they won 3–1 at Middlesbrough, their first away win of the season.

Afterwards, assistant boss Jim Smith paid tribute to his side's newest striking sensation, who took his tally to ten goals in his last 13 games with his brace at the Riverside Stadium. Smith said in an interview with the club's website, 'I had seen him [Crouch] on TV with Pompey and a bit with Villa, but it was only when I got to work with him that I realised just how good he is.

'Everyone just thinks of him as a big target man, and his pure size does mean he's a handful, but I've been amazed by his ability on the ball. His goal record is excellent, and he's going to get more now he has people who believe in him.'

That win took Saints out of the bottom three, with Smith hailing it as 'a massive win for us, possibly the defining moment of the season'. The fact that they overhauled Palace suggested that Smith's words might just come true, but just as it looked as though there was light at the end of tunnel, the wheels fell off.

Southampton lost their next two matches – at home to champions elect Chelsea and away to Blackburn – meaning that they had slipped back into the relegation zone by the time the next visitors arrived at St Mary's. And those visitors were Aston Villa.

You would have thought Crouch would have been desperate to prove that Villa boss O'Leary had been wrong to reject him but, on the eve of the match, he insisted, 'There are no grudges on my part. But it was time for me to move on. I just felt I was not going to play because the manager fancied other players, which is fair enough. That happens in football.'

Crouch may have felt he had nothing to prove to the Villa management, but it was clear that he had decided to let his feet do the talking for him. Remarkably, as the two sides prepared to meet at St Mary's, it became apparent that Crouch had scored more goals on his own than the entire Villa strike-force put together.

His 13 goals were more than Juan Pablo Angel, Darius Vassell and Carlton Cole had managed between them – a damning statistic if ever there was one. But O'Leary remained defiant.

He told the *Star*, 'Peter's a lovely boy and he always did a job for us whenever we needed him, but letting him go was in everyone's best interests. He wanted to play regular first-team football and Angel and Vassell were always going to play for us. We took money for him, which helped us sign Martin Laursen.

'I know people will criticise me because he's scoring some goals, but he's a centre-forward and I didn't sell him thinking he would never score again. I shook hands with him and wished him all the best and, if we both have long careers, I'm sure he'll score against me sooner rather than later. I'm sure I will probably have that thrown in my face.'

It took Crouch just 13 minutes to prove O'Leary right – or wrong, as the case may be – as he scored Southampton's second goal of the afternoon as they raced into a 2–0 lead. They could not have wished for a better start but, as had happened so often during the season, things went rapidly downhill from there on.

This time, however, there was not the agony of three points turning into one, but of three points turning into none. Carlton Cole, Nolberto Solano and Steven Davis all netted for Villa in a nightmare second half for Southampton as they crumbled to a hugely damaging defeat.

Manager Redknapp confessed in his post-match press conference, 'We've got it all to do now. That was a massive blow. We needed three points. We stood off them and let them play. It should have been over at half-time as we were absolutely fantastic in the first half. We controlled the game, looked great up front and were special. It was nothing to do with complacency; it's the nerve that goes. It's going to be really hard now.'

Southampton picked themselves up from that demoralising setback to pick up a point in their next match, away at Bolton, which meant that, with four games remaining, they were one point behind West Bromwich Albion and safety.

The fact that two of those matches were against the only two sides below them, Norwich and Crystal Palace, and that the other one was against the team in 16th place, Portsmouth, gave everyone at the club hope that salvation could still be achieved.

The first game of that final quartet meant an emotionally charged return to Fratton Park for Redknapp, and for Crouch. And, of course, the Pompey fans still had bitter memories of the striker's last-minute penalty winner that had ended their FA Cup hopes just three months previously.

However, far from being intimidated by the short trip along the south coast, Crouch was relishing it. He told the *Sun*, 'I try to keep it quiet that I was at Portsmouth, even though I had a good time there. I know I might get a hot reception there, but to be honest I get stick from opposition fans every week anyway.

'Having been tall all my life, I'm an obvious target, so it will be no different at Pompey. It's a game I'm really looking forward to. Up until now we have just been looking at the bottom four clubs in the relegation picture, but now we want to drag Portsmouth into it.

'Palace, West Brom and ourselves have been picking up points and we are dragging people in. With Portsmouth losing at Fulham last weekend, we believe we can pull them in.

'It's going to be a huge game at Fratton Park. We've had a couple of good results against them at St Mary's this season and I scored the winner in the FA Cup match, so we'll be confident.

'I know the derby means so much to everyone, but considering it might be make or break whether both sides stay in the Premiership, this one is going to be even more exciting.

'We can see light at the end of the tunnel. Since Harry Redknapp brought five new players in during January, they have freshened things up and have real presence in the dressing room.'

But there was to be a crushing blow both for Crouch and Redknapp before the match had even kicked off when Crouch injured his hamstring in the pre-match warm-up and had to pull out.

But surely no one could have foreseen that Crouch's withdrawal would demoralise his team-mates to such an extent that they would slump to a humiliating 4–1 defeat – their heaviest ever defeat at Fratton Park in arguably the most crucial derby game ever staged between the two teams.

It left them with a huge mountain to climb if they were to avoid the drop and Redknapp admitted as much afterwards: 'If we keep conceding goals like that, we've got no chance. This is as big a hole as I have ever been in – and if we can't beat Norwich next week then we are probably gone.

'It is going to take three wins now. That is difficult but not impossible and we can still do it. I've got to try and pick this team up. But I don't know who is going to motivate me.'

Wherever he found the motivation to keep himself going through the following week ahead of the Norwich game, find it he did. And he was rewarded with an astonishing performance in one of the matches of the season.

Crouch had recovered from his hamstring pull to take his place in the starting line-up against the team that had done so much to restore his confidence during his three months at Carrow Road. But, with both teams desperate for points as they sought to survive and condemn the other to the drop, there was no room for sentiment.

An incredible first half saw Southampton lead twice and Norwich once before they went in level at the break having shared six goals – Crouch having scored his side's second, and the third of the match, in the 20th minute.

Remarkably, given the goal-fest that had taken place before the interval, there were no further goals until two minutes from time when Henri Camara struck to settle a nerve-tingling encounter and revive hopes of a miracle escape act for the Saints.

Redknapp could not contain his delight as he addressed the post-match press conference. He said, 'We had to win the game and the lads showed a hell of a lot of character to come back and get the victory. It is wrong that we have to score four goals to win a match at the moment, but we played some terrific stuff going forward. It was tense stuff, but we have given ourselves a fighting chance.'

The Saints boss also heaped praise on Crouch, who took the decision himself to gamble on the fitness of his hamstring, and called for him to be called up for international duty. Redknapp said, 'I would have him in the England squad – he could be a great substitute for them. He would be someone you could have on the bench who offers you something different.

'There are going to be games where you can't break teams down and can't play through them with small strikers. When you bring on a guy who's 6ft 7in, it gives you extra options.'

For now, though, England would have to wait. With just two games remaining, the Saints were out of the bottom three, albeit on goal difference, with just one point separating the bottom four. And, with Chelsea having long since wrapped up their first league title in 50 years, the country's entire focus was on the battle at the basement.

Next up was a trip to Crystal Palace, the side immediately below them. And no one at St Mary's needed reminding of just how important the game was to the club's future.

Goalkeeper Antti Niemi told the club's website, 'It is going to be a huge game. Whoever wins this will make it hugely difficult for the losers to stay up. I have played in some big matches at this club, like the FA Cup final and in the UEFA Cup, but I would say this is bigger than both of them. For the long-term future of the club, this is much more important.'

The game at Selhurst Park may not have been quite as thrilling as the previous week's clash with Norwich, but there was not much to choose between the two sides. Fitz Hall gave Palace the lead in the 34th minute, only for Crouch to equalise from the penalty spot just three minutes later. Nicola Ventola restored the home side's advantage with just 18 minutes left, before defender Danny Higginbotham's last-minute intervention saw Southampton rescue a point in dramatic fashion.

By then, however, Crouch was already showered and changed having been sent off just before the hour mark. He was dismissed for a clash with Gonzalo Sorondo, but Redknapp was furious with referee Howard Webb's decision to brandish a red card.

After the match, the Saints boss fumed, 'With the sending off, we lost a key player and they lost a right-back! The referee told both players they would get a yellow card, but then spoke to the linesman and the fourth official and sent them both off!

'I will have a look at the replay and, if there is a reason to appeal, then we will. We will miss him as he is an important player and a good footballer.'

The situation at the bottom could hardly have been closer. Just two points separated the bottom four and all of the sides could still stay up or go down.

Norwich were in the best position, knowing that a win in their final match at Fulham would make them safe, irrespective of what happened elsewhere. Not in their favour, though, was the fact that they had yet to win a Premiership match on their travels during the course of the season.

Crystal Palace faced a trip to south London rivals Charlton, while West Brom, who started the final day in bottom spot, played host to Portsmouth. The toughest task, undoubtedly, was the one facing Southampton, as they entertained a Manchester United side that was still in a battle with Arsenal for second place and the remaining automatic Champions League place.

And it was a Manchester United side that just eight weeks previously had thrashed the Saints on their own patch to book their place in the FA Cup semi-finals.

Redknapp, though, remained convinced his side would survive, telling journalists after the Palace draw, 'I still think we will do it. We are still in there, we can do it and it's all to play for. I believe in fate and I just feel we are destined to stay up.'

After studying video footage, Southampton decided to launch an appeal against Crouch's red card in a bid to ensure he would be available for the crucial encounter with United. Everyone at the club was desperate to see it succeed.

Goalkeeper Niemi admitted Crouch's absence would be a huge blow. 'If we had known on Saturday that we would end up playing ten against ten, he [Crouch] would have been the last player we would have wanted to lose,' the Finnish international told the club's website.

He added, 'It's not just his goals; if things aren't going your way he gives you that option and you can play the ball up to him. He holds the ball up and he sucks in defenders around him.

'At the start of the season when we signed him, there were quite a few people who doubted his ability.

He was starting on the bench and sometimes he wasn't even in the squad at all. But in my eyes he has been our best player this season and it will be a big blow to be without him.'

But without him they were, after the FA rejected the appeal and upheld his three-match ban. Redknapp, while disappointed, remained philosophical. He said of the verdict, 'Peter will be a big miss because he has been magnificent for us this season, but we have some terrific other front players. Whoever plays will be ready and will give it everything. All the players know the importance of this one.'

The disappointment for Crouch in missing out on such a key fixture was huge. But in a week of contrasting emotions, he was given a massive boost when he was named in the senior England squad for the first time.

However, although naturally delighted to be selected for the post-season tour of the USA, he insisted that he would gladly swap personal honours for team success. He told Southampton's website, 'I am absolutely delighted to be in the squad, but I would trade it for us staying up – and that's the truth.

'Survival means so much to the club, the city and the fans, and it will be so frustrating watching the match from the stands and kicking every ball. It will be hard not being part of it, but I'm confident the lads will win the game.

'I was gutted to be sent off, and knowing that I can't affect such a vital match is really hard to take. The appeal was always going to be a long shot, but we had to try because I was desperate to play.

'This news [of my call-up] has given me a lift, though, and I just hope it is a good omen for us. Hopefully it will be a really good week.'

Crouch, who had previously represented his country at Under-18 and Under-21 levels, admitted that selection for Sven-Goran Eriksson's senior party had come sooner than he would have expected.

He added, 'It's probably come a bit earlier than I would have thought, especially as I was not even in the Southampton side at the start of the season. But I always felt confident that if I got a run of games then I could do well. The manager has given me a chance and I hope I have repaid him.

'He said a couple of days ago that he thought I could get in this squad, but it was still a surprise when the news came. It is a great honour.'

But sadly, for Crouch and Southampton, there was to be no happy ending to the week. They made the best possible start to the final game, taking the lead after just ten minutes thanks to a John O'Shea own goal but, as had happened so often throughout the season, they were unable to hold on to the lead.

Darren Fletcher levelled the scores in the 19th minute, and Ruud van Nistelrooy hammered the final nail into the relegation coffin with the winning goal 23 minutes before the end.

To add to their misery, there was the knowledge that it could have been very different. Norwich – the only team at the bottom who held their Premiership survival in their own hands – were thrashed at Fulham, while Crystal Palace could manage only a draw against Charlton. And so it was West Bromwich Albion, courtesy of victory over, ironically, Portsmouth, who stayed up.

Had Southampton beaten United, it would have been they, not Albion, who survived. Instead, they not only went down, they also suffered the ignominy of finishing bottom of the table.

Despite the disappointment, however, manager Redknapp remained bullish and was resolute in his determination that the club would recover and would return better and stronger than before. He vowed, 'This club will come back up, there is no doubt about that.'

However, during the course of the same press conference, it appeared that he was actually starting to have doubts. Far from continuing to bang the drum, he admitted, 'There is a need to improve in certain areas and there are far too many players and not enough quality.

'I have never seen so many players at one club – I don't know where they have all come from. I suppose it is because managers have come and gone and brought their own players in, but there needs to be major surgery. It needs a mass clear-out and some new blood.'

The first thing Redknapp had to thrash out, though, was his own future. With just a year left on his contract, he had hinted that he might retire from football altogether if the Saints were relegated but, within days of the club's demotion, it soon became apparent that he was poised to stay.

Following a meeting with chairman Lowe, he told the club's website, 'We had a nice positive chat and there is no doubt about me wanting to stay. I have enjoyed my time here, it is a good club. I want to stay, but I needed to sit down with the chairman to talk about next season.

'I feel it is important to try to hang on to our best players, and then maybe add one or two so that we can make a meaningful challenge. I wanted to make sure there was not going to be a wholesale fire-sale of players, because we will need them to get back up.

'We both want the same thing – to get this club back in the Premier League.'

One of those players Redknapp was desperate to keep hold of was Crouch. He insisted, 'He is going to be a key player for us next season. We have not had any offers yet, and, if someone offers ridiculous money, then that's football. But in an ideal world I would want to keep him. He had a great second half to the season for us after I gave him his chance and I'm sure he can do the same again.

'If Norwich are keeping Dean Ashton and Palace are keeping Andy Johnson, then we need to keep Peter Crouch, who has turned out to be a fantastic player. He is a very, very key player and the sort we need to keep and build a team around.'

And that stance was backed up by Lowe, who insisted, 'Peter Crouch is not for sale. He has been outstanding this season and we want him to stay and bring us back up.'

But while Southampton were planning for life in the Championship and Crouch's future was being discussed by the power brokers at St Mary's, the striker himself was 6,000 miles away in America preparing for his England debut.

A memorable season, one which had seen him score 15 goals in just 24 starts, culminated in his winning

Southampton's Player of the Season award by a landslide margin. Voted for by readers of the local *Daily Echo* newspaper, he won by one of the biggest majorities since the award's inauguration in 1974, polling a massive 84.75 per cent of the votes.

That relegated the previous year's winner, Antti Niemi, into second place, with Crouch's strike partner Kevin Phillips coming in third. Those two, however, polled just 4.66 per cent and 3.38 per cent of the vote, respectively.

Although nothing could make up for the heartbreak of relegation, it must have come as some consolation to Crouch that the fans recognised the huge part he had played in the club's failed survival battle. And so, despite the team's woe, he could approach his first England tour full of confidence.

Manager Sven-Goran Eriksson named a youthful squad for the end-of-season tour which was to feature games against the USA and Colombia. Although Crouch was the only player called up for the first time, other so-called fringe players selected included the likes of Glen Johnson, Matthew Upson, Stewart Downing, Shaun Wright-Phillips and Andy Johnson.

And the Swede singled out Crouch for praise at his press conference to announce his tour party. He said, 'He's different, very different. When you go into a big tournament, you should have one big striker.

'If you put the ball up there, he will win it. His touch is not bad at all and, if you are trying everything in the last 15 minutes to break them [the opposition] down, then maybe you could put on Peter Crouch. I'm not saying that I will definitely do it, but I will look at him in America.'

One man who was certainly not shocked that Crouch had received a full international call-up was his former QPR boss Gerry Francis. He told the *Evening Standard*, 'I'm not surprised England have called him up. I think you'll find he'll be a big name in the game. You get the jokes about his size, but he can play. He reminds me of Teddy Sheringham with his ability and thinking.

'He's not the quickest until he gets into his stride, but he has great technique. You can put it into his feet, he has a great touch and he's scored some fantastic volleys. He's got the build of Niall Quinn and no one can handle him if he jumps.

'He'll be very hard to play against if he fills out and gets stronger. Some international teams will not know what has hit them and a really good striker working off him will get a lot of goals.'

By the time the tour got started, Eriksson's squad had an even more unfamiliar look about it. With the likes of Rio Ferdinand, John Terry, Steven Gerrard, Frank Lampard and Wayne Rooney not considered for selection, it was already sure to be an experimental line-up.

And, when injuries struck before the action even got under way, Eriksson drafted in Kieron Richardson, Zat Knight and Luke Young, ensuring that there would be several debuts handed out during the trip. The Swede had already talked of his intention to hand Crouch his first senior cap, but the player himself admitted he had mixed feelings about the trip, tinged as it was with sadness following Southampton's relegation.

'It was a massive boost for me to come away with

England, but to be relegated left me gutted, especially for me, as I was not involved on the last day of the season,' he told thefa.com. 'It was hard to take, watching the lads go down, and I felt guilty about being sent off the week before. We left ourselves a big task playing United in the final game, but as it worked out we would have stayed up if we had won, so it is hard to take.'

Crouch, of course, had had previous England experience in the junior ranks, playing for both the Under-18s and Under-21s, but confessed, 'At the start of the season I would have said, "You're mad" if you had said I would be on an England tour at the end of it. But things happen quickly in football. In the second half of the season I hit a good vein of goal-scoring form and thought I was playing as well as I have ever played.

'If you look at the strikers in the England squad at the moment, I am definitely unique. I'm different to a lot of the other strikers here. I bring something different and I think that's what the manager is looking for.'

But Crouch was also keen to stress that he was more than just a big target man. He added, 'My height is an asset. But I'd like to think I can hold the ball up well and bring other players into play as well. If it is hard to break teams down, then I am a different option. It is not just about lumping the ball into me.

'This season I've scored as many goals with my feet as with my head and I'd like to think there are two sides to my game. I feel I've got to perform in these two games to stake a real claim for a place.

'There are a lot of players unavailable, but I am a unique striker and the manager has been quoted as saying he wants a bigger player alongside the other strikers. I'm hoping to fill that gap.

'I'll be trying my utmost to impress this week, but the manager has pulled me to one side and said, "Don't feel nervous or under pressure," because he can watch me all of next season as well. Now I am involved with England, I want to be a part of it all the time.'

Eriksson's words of encouragement for Crouch were also good news for Southampton. The England boss reassured the striker that playing in the Championship would not harm his international chances, nor would it damage his prospects of being selected for the 2006 World Cup finals.

Crouch told Southampton's website, 'It was good to hear that [from Eriksson]. I've got to speak with the chairman and with Harry Redknapp, but I imagine I will be with Southampton next season.

'It is flattering to be linked with clubs like Liverpool and it shows I have done my job this season, but I do want to settle down. I do want to cement something. That's not to say that playing in the Championship won't be difficult – it will be. There is no denying it. We were all desperate to stay in the Premiership, especially myself.

'I will speak to the club, but at the moment I believe I will be at Southampton next season.'

For now, though, uppermost in Crouch's thoughts was not the following season's domestic campaign, but the two games in the USA and the chance to stake his claim for a regular place in the national squad.

And it soon became clear that he was going to be given that chance in the first match when he was named in the starting line-up to face the USA in Chicago. However, there was to be more misery for the young man still struggling to deal with the reality of relegation.

Just as he was looking forward to his senior England debut – and, incidentally, a place in the record books as his country's tallest ever player – he was ruled out following a training-ground injury he picked up in a challenge with Sol Campbell.

He could only watch from the bench and wonder what might have been as England ran out 2–1 winners, thanks to a brace from Manchester United midfielder Richardson on his debut, a player who had not even been named in the original touring squad.

That left Crouch with the task of proving his fitness in the three days before the match against Colombia if he was to avoid the disappointment of missing out on his debut. And, as any player will stress, no matter what they might be being told by the manager about future opportunities, if they are given a chance they know they have to take it. With constant uncertainties surrounding form and fitness, there are no guarantees that such an opportunity will ever come again.

Fortunately for Crouch, his recovery appeared to go smoothly. He told the FA's website, 'I had doubts about whether I would make it or not, but I've come through training fine. I will put ice on the ankle again, but I am sure I will be fit.

'This is a big lift for me because I was devastated [to miss the American game]. It is not every day you get a chance to make your England debut and to miss out against America was a big blow. Psychologically it was devastating. I was named in the starting XI and then ruled out because of a silly little injury in training.'

Having recovered sufficiently, Crouch was duly named in the team to face Colombia. And, in a further boost, he was named up front alongside Michael Owen, who had sat out the USA victory having arrived from Spain after the rest of the party, along with his Real Madrid team-mate David Beckham.

And the 'Little and Large' pairing in attack hit it off straight away. Owen grabbed the headlines with a hat-trick in the 3–2 win over the South Americans, but there was enough evidence in their striking partnership to suggest it could be a profitable one for England.

That was never more obvious than for Owen's second goal, when Crouch spotted his clever run and slid a quick pass into his partner's path that Owen finished with typical aplomb.

Two wins from two games with an under-strength squad, and impressive performances from newcomers like Crouch, Richardson and Michael Carrick, made it an encouraging trip for Eriksson with the World Cup a little over 12 months away. Of Crouch, the England manager said, 'I liked what I saw.'

The Swede added, 'You can't defend in the air against him – it is impossible – and he has good feet as well. If you give him the ball, he does not give it away.'

Eriksson's flattering comments were a further boost for Crouch after the disappointing end to the domestic season. And having demonstrated that he could cut the mustard at international level, and proved conclusively that he could score goals at the highest level of English football, again in a struggling side, he returned home from America to find another manager singing his praises.

This one was a little closer to home and perhaps not quite as exotic as the FA's favourite foreign coach, but nonetheless Harry Redknapp's fierce determination to keep Crouch at St Mary's would have been music to the ears of a player who, by now, people were surely realising responded best when he was surrounded by people who believed in him.

With the vultures circling Southampton ready to pick the bones out of Redknapp's squad, the Saints boss reiterated his desire to retain Crouch's services. He insisted to the local media, 'I sold him once at Portsmouth, and it was a lot of money at the time, but it is not something I would do again. Even if someone came in with the same money, I wouldn't take it. What would you do with it?

'I couldn't put a price on him and I don't want to either because I don't want to sell him. It is as simple as that. It is going to be a very tough division next year and if you want to get out of it you've got to keep your best players. Keeping Crouch is vital. He is our trump card.'

Crouch's performances for club and country, though, had alerted him to the footballing fraternity at large, and it was becoming obvious that Southampton were facing a real battle to hang on to him.

Liverpool were reportedly the first to test the water, with an offer thought to be in the region of £5 million. Chairman Lowe would not confirm the identity of the bidding club, but stressed to the Southampton website, 'We do not discuss our transfer business, but there has been a lot of interest in Peter Crouch. And we have had an offer which we have turned down.'

Crouch's former club Tottenham were also linked with a move for the striker, and the speculation was beginning to take its toll on Redknapp. After national newspaper reports that he was fighting a losing battle to keep hold of his star striker following showdown talks between the pair, Redknapp insisted, 'The story is absolute rubbish. I don't know where it has come from.'

He added on the club's website, 'I am in Sardinia, so quite how I am supposed to have had talks with him I don't know!'

As the summer continued, though, the speculation scarcely abated as the rumour mill continued to turn. Redknapp was still insisting that he was not interested in any deal for Crouch, and he was also appealing to the player to show some loyalty to the club that had rescued him from his nightmare at Aston Villa, and to the manager who had shown so much faith in him in the second half of the season.

'I would like to think he owes it to us,' Redknapp told the club's website. 'He was not playing much up until Christmas, but I put him in the team and he had a good half season. But he still has a long way to go and I think it would do him the world of good to stay and get us back up.'

The transfer talk continued throughout the close season but, when Southampton returned for pre-season training in early July, Crouch was still there. However, the rumours persisted, with West Ham, Manchester City and, of course, Liverpool all having been linked with fresh moves for him in the Sunday newspapers the previous weekend.

But Saints fans must have been thinking that, against all the odds, they would succeed in keeping Crouch, just as Crystal Palace had refused to budge in their assertion that they would not let Andy Johnson leave.

As the players returned to training, Redknapp told the club's website, 'It has been well documented that Liverpool came in for Crouch and I can understand that he wants to play at the top level and be involved in Champions League football. But I don't think it makes any difference which division he is playing in, as long as he is playing well I still think he will be in the World Cup squad.'

But still the bids kept coming. And still Southampton turned them down. And still Redknapp insisted that the player was not for sale.

Liverpool and West Ham both had £6 million offers rejected, but the problems for Southampton were worsening. The money being talked about was going up – and the player himself was starting to become unsettled.

A clause in his contract meant that his wages had been halved following relegation, reportedly to £4,000 a week, and, with Liverpool said to be ready to offer him £30,000 a week, Crouch was starting to get restless.

Redknapp admitted on saintsfc.com, 'Let's be honest, Peter Crouch wants to play for Liverpool. Let's not kid ourselves. And I can understand where he is coming from. He can get eight times what he earns here and play in the Champions League. He knows I understand his situation and it is not easy for me to tell him he is not leaving, but I have a job to do.

'I have to look after the good of the club. Peter can say what he wants, but he's got a contract here.'

Crouch played in Southampton's first pre-season friendly as they set about preparing for their Championship campaign, but his lacklustre display in a 2–1 win at Motherwell led to fresh rumours that it would be his last game in a Saints shirt before the completion of his much-talked-about move to Merseyside.

But his display in the second game of that Scottish tour certainly silenced any of his doubters, as he emerged from the bench at half-time to score twice in the final nine minutes to earn Southampton a 3–2 win over Kilmarnock.

And Redknapp was quick to hail his star striker's contribution and his commitment. 'Peter took his goals well and showed a good attitude, despite all the stuff that is going on,' he told the Saints website.

'It cannot be easy for him with all the transfer speculation and with him wanting to go to Liverpool. But he is a great lad and a terrific pro. I just hope Liverpool don't come in with an increased bid.'

But when Charlton and Middlesbrough then reportedly joined the race, with Manchester City still in the hunt and now ready to spend some of the £21 million Chelsea had just handed them for Shaun Wright-Phillips, Redknapp's worst fears were confirmed.

Liverpool moved swiftly to see off the competition and tie up a £7 million deal, with Crouch agreeing a four-year contract. Rafael Benitez's patient pursuit of his number-one transfer target had paid off.

For Redknapp, there was only disappointment. He

admitted, 'I would love to have kept him. He was a key player and he is a good lad, too. Throughout all of this, he has been as good as gold, and I'm sure he will be a big success there.'

For all his frustrations at failing to keep the one player he valued above all others, however, you suspect that Redknapp, one of British football's arch exponents of the transfer market, always knew that, no matter how many battles he won throughout the summer, he would end up losing the war.

And he was typically philosophical when he said, 'It was too good an offer. You cannot turn down £7 million for a player who you would not have paid £700,000 for six months ago!'

Ultimately, no matter how much they wanted to keep him, once Crouch had had his head turned by Liverpool, they were always going to struggle to keep him. At that stage, when it becomes clear that the player has made up his mind to leave, clubs accept it and then do their utmost to get the best possible price. That is exactly what Southampton did.

It was a dream move for Crouch, but he was quick to pay tribute to the man who made it possible – Harry Redknapp. He told local journalists, 'I am grateful to Harry for everything he has done for me in my career to date. He made it clear he would not stand in my way over this transfer move.

'The chairman has also handled the negotiations with me and the other clubs professionally and fairly and I would like to thank both of them for the way they have conducted themselves during these discussions. I would also like to thank all the Southampton fans for their support and wish them all the best for the season.

'I am thrilled to be joining a club as prestigious as Liverpool. Once I heard of their interest in me, it was hard not to think about what it would be like to pull on the famous red shirt and play in front of the Kop, but I was also very aware of my responsibilities towards Southampton.

'After a lot of thought I requested permission from the chairman and the board of directors to talk to Liverpool. Southampton bought me from Aston Villa and allowed me to play regularly in the Premiership which resulted in an appearance for England in the summer.

'This has helped my career tremendously and has now given me the opportunity to move to Liverpool and play on an even bigger stage, something that no one could realistically expect me to turn down. Under almost any other circumstances, I would have committed to helping Southampton regain their Premiership status.'

CHAPTER 5

HITTING THE BIG TIME

As the days ticked down towards the start of the 2005–06 season and as Southampton prepared for the challenge of trying to regain their place in the Premiership at the first attempt, Crouch was readying himself for life at Anfield – the fourth time in five years that he had started the season at a new club – and all the challenges that move would bring. After all, you could argue that no club in England has the history and tradition of Liverpool's.

From the days of Bill Shankly in the 1960s, through the Bob Paisley era in the mid-1970s to the mid-1980s, to the continued glory days under Joe Fagan and Kenny Dalglish, the club enjoyed an unprecedented run of success.

During that period, between 1970 and 1990, the club amassed an extraordinary 31 major trophies, including an incredible 13 League Championships (their overall tally of

18 remains the most by any English league side) and four European Cup triumphs. They were, without question, the most successful club side in Europe.

But the league title had eluded them for the past 16 years, something that would have been unthinkable back then. Graeme Souness, Roy Evans and Gerard Houllier, and at one stage a combination of the latter two, all tried and failed to end that miserable run, before the baton was passed to Spaniard Rafael Benitez in the summer of 2004.

His first season in charge saw the club finish in a disappointing fifth spot in the league, equalling their worst finish in six years. Worse, they ended up below Merseyside rivals Everton, who finished one place above them. But Liverpool fans did have the massive consolation of winning the Champions League – against all the odds – particularly in the final against AC Milan in Istanbul where they recovered from a 3–0 half-time deficit to win the giant European trophy for a fifth time, after a penalty shoot-out.

So Crouch found himself at a club on a new high on his first day as he set about the task of following in the footsteps of legendary Liverpool strikers such as Roger Hunt and Ian St John, John Toshack and Kevin Keegan, Ian Rush and Kenny Dalglish and, more recently, Robbie Fowler and Michael Owen.

That is a tall order for any forward, but his new manager and team-mates were convinced that Crouch had the ability to deliver the goods.

On the player's first day at the club, Benitez told reporters, 'I'm delighted we have signed him. He is a good player with a lot of qualities and his arrival will give me more options up front. He got goals in a struggling side and, although it's a different pressure at Liverpool, hopefully he will cope with it.

'We had trouble controlling him last season. It was the first part of last season when I first noticed Crouch. I saw some videos of him in action and I immediately thought to myself that he was a good player.

'I spoke to our scouting department about him and we watched him over the remainder of the season. Of course, in our away game at Southampton last season we had problems controlling him. We didn't play very well that day and one of the reasons for that was Peter Crouch.

'Another reason I like him is because he is English. It is always important to bring English players to the club, but only at the right price – I think we have done a good deal for Liverpool.'

England defender Jamie Carragher also remembered Crouch's impact during that game at St Mary's, and he was delighted that he was about to have the big striker on his side rather than have to face him again, rating him second only to Arsenal superstar Thierry Henry in his list of toughest opponents.

He revealed in the *Evening Standard*, 'Besides Henry, in the second half of last season Crouchy was probably as good as any striker in the Premiership. When he played at Southampton against us last season, that performance alone was probably sufficient to get him a move here, never mind anything else.

'He's just very, very hard to handle. I found him a nightmare. He scored at the back post and got in behind me, so it was probably my fault! He did play incredibly well in that game and he was the one who really gave Southampton a chance of staying up.

'I watch a lot of football and every time I saw him play he was outstanding, no matter who he was up against, even the top teams. His suspension towards the end of the season was probably what cost Southampton.

'Obviously he brings aerial ability because of his size. But he has much more than that, he has real technique. I know a lot of the lads at Southampton – Jamie Redknapp is a close friend – and he's been raving about him for six months. He says he really can play.'

And it wasn't only the current crop of Liverpool stars who rated their new colleague. Former Anfield greats were also delighted to see Crouch brought to the club. One of those was Jimmy Case, a midfield powerhouse who won a stack of medals with the club in the 1970s and early 1980s.

He felt that Crouch could bring a similar dimension to the current side as Toshack had brought to the team all those years ago. He told the *Liverpool Echo*, 'I am an admirer of Peter Crouch and think he is a good signing for Liverpool. He played ever so well for Southampton last season and he is very good on the ball for such a big guy.

'He can win the ball, hold it up and bring others into play. He has a very good awareness about him and playing in the Liverpool team will only improve him as a player as he is still learning and not the finished article yet.

'A lot of people might be surprised that Rafael Benitez wanted him so much, but it's all about fitting in with the manager's thoughts and I think he will be a good signing for my old club.

'We had Toshack, who was a big lad, and Kevin Keegan up front and they did pretty well, didn't they! I'm not saying Crouch is the new John Toshack or anything like that, but he is a good player and I think he will be a success for Liverpool.

'I've watched Peter since he played at Portsmouth and, if you are looking for a striker who is going to cause defences havoc, who can score goals, and who brings others into play, then there's nothing better around than Peter Crouch.'

Crouch himself couldn't wait to get started. 'Liverpool are traditionally the biggest club in England and I've just come in on the back of a Champions League win. It's been manic, the fans are so passionate and now they have even higher expectations,' he said in an interview with *Shoot Monthly*.

'We may have won the Champions League last year, but there was still a big gap in the Premiership between us and Chelsea. We need to close that gap. With the players the manager has brought in, we can do that.

'We have some great players like Steven Gerrard and Xabi Alonso, and, once the new players gel, we'll be looking to close that gap. It may take a little time, but we can only get stronger and stronger.

'The manager has said I'm a good player and that I can fit into the side quickly and well. I think he sees my strengths both playing up front on my own or with a partner, giving the side different options.

'People who hadn't seen me play said I was only good

in the air, but I think that's starting to change now. People realise now I can play on the floor, as well as my height being an advantage. The manager and players here realise that my passing game is also a big part of me and that I can set things up in that way.

'The manager wants to compete for everything and he's not just going to bring in someone that the other players can lump the ball up to. I've got to play to the team's strengths, which are passing and moving. I know I can do that, as does the manager. With the quality we have in the team we can pass it as well as the best of them.

'I see similarities between myself and Niall Quinn – there's not many of us about! He had a great touch and could bring others into the game. I can do that, too.

'I'm getting better each season. If I'm playing regularly, I'll also get physically stronger and there's definitely a lot more to come from me. And now I have the privilege of showing what I can do on the biggest possible stage.'

Crouch's first taste of life in a Liverpool shirt came in the second qualifying round of the Champions League at the end of July 2005. Having won the trophy just two months before, but finished outside the top four in the Premiership, the Reds had been forced to plead their case with UEFA before finally being allowed to defend their trophy.

Their 'punishment' was being made to pre-qualify for the tournament so, having already seen off the challenge of Welsh part-timers Total Network Solutions in the first qualifying round, without Crouch, it was in the unfamiliar setting of Lithuania, against FBK Kaunas, that he made his Liverpool debut.

It was a comfortable enough night's work for the defending champions, although they did have to come from 1–0 down to win 3–1. For his part, Crouch played an encouraging 74 minutes, including setting up the equaliser for Djibril Cisse, before Fernando Morientes replaced him.

A week later, Liverpool made certain of their passage to the third qualifying round with a 2–0 second-leg win over the Lithuanians, but the performance was less than convincing. On this occasion, Crouch played 55 minutes before Darren Potter came on as his replacement. Both goals, from Steven Gerrard and Cisse, came in the last 13 minutes.

Crouch would clearly have loved to have opened his goal account for his new club in one of those European matches, particularly as his sending-off against Crystal Palace at the back end of the previous season meant that he would be suspended for the first two Premiership games of the new season.

Bearing that in mind, it came as no real surprise that Benitez opted to play Cisse and Fernando Morientes up front in the first leg of the Champions League third qualifying round, away to CSKA Sofia – a match Liverpool won 3–1 with the twin strike-force responsible for all three goals, Cisse scoring once and his Spanish partner netting a brace.

While that was, of course, good for the team, it merely increased the pressure on Crouch to ensure he took his chance the next time it came around.

Sandwiched between the two legs of that European tie against the Bulgarians was the start of the new Premiership season. And as Liverpool prepared to kick off the domestic campaign at Middlesbrough, a game that would be their sixth competitive fixture of the season having begun exactly a month earlier on 13 July against TNS, Benitez spoke confidently of his side's hopes of challenging champions Chelsea for the title.

With Crouch just one of six new signings during the summer – the others being Jose Reina, Bolo Zenden, Momo Sissoko, Mark Gonzales and Antonio Barragan – the Spaniard was in a bullish mood.

'We knew we needed to improve the quality of the squad and that is what we have done. We needed to strengthen different positions and we're happy with the players we have managed to bring in,' he told the *Liverpool Post*.

'I have been here for a year now with my staff and we all have more experience of English football. I wanted to sign some players with experience of the Premiership and we've done that in Zenden and Crouch. We have more quality to work with now and so I am sure we will do better in the league. That's our idea.

'We have more options for different positions in the team and so the competition for places is going to be strong. All the players are working as hard as they can in pre-season and in the friendly games to show me they are worth a place in the side. We probably still need to strengthen certain positions in the squad and that is something we are working on at the moment.'

For all the confident words, though, the season did not start in quite the fashion Benitez would have wanted. A disappointing 0–0 draw at Middlesbrough on the opening day was followed by a not altogether convincing

1–0 win over Premiership new boys Sunderland at Anfield a week later.

And when the side slipped to a 1–0 home defeat against Sofia in the return leg of their Champions League qualifier three days after that – a loss that fortunately wasn't too damaging given the 3–1 scoreline from the first leg – the first signs that all was perhaps not quite right, particularly in the malfunctioning forward line, started to appear.

Crouch, of course, had been unable to play a part in any of those matches, and he also sat out the UEFA Super Cup final in Monaco against CSKA Moscow, as Liverpool's already crowded fixture list continued to get more and more congested. However, they did have the bonus of winning that match 3–1, and both the victory and goals (two for Cisse and one for Luis Garcia) would certainly have given the squad a much-needed confidence boost.

They had played four games in less than two weeks though – two in domestic competition and two in Europe – and Benitez now had to face up to his players disappearing to all four corners of the globe to play for their countries.

For Crouch and his fellow England team-mates at Anfield, the journey was only a short one as they faced back-to-back World Cup qualifiers at home to Austria and Poland, games that were to be played at Manchester United's Old Trafford ground and that would go a long way to determining England's fate in the qualification campaign.

However, the international break meant that, when the

Liverpool players returned to Melwood, the club's training ground, there was almost a sense of them starting the season again.

The international break had come at a bad time for the Liverpool squad. After an unconvincing start to the campaign, Benitez would surely have preferred to have kept his players closer to home to work on things in a bid to improve on their slightly faltering start, even though four points from two games hardly represented a disaster.

The next game saw Liverpool travel to Tottenham, meaning a return to his first club for Crouch. The game also marked his Premiership debut for his new club, and his first real chance to show the doubters that he was worthy of the £7 million price tag.

And with the game locked level at 0–0 after 69 minutes, it appeared as though he had done it as he headed home Gerrard's corner to give Liverpool the lead and mark his first Premiership start for his new club with his first goal for them.

His joy was to be short-lived, however, as the referee's assistant indicated that Gerrard's flag kick had drifted out of play before reaching Crouch's 6ft 7in frame. Incredibly, just eight minutes earlier, Tottenham's Grzegorz Rasiak had had a debut goal of his own ruled out for exactly the same reason. At the time, however, no one could have known just how much that linesman's decision would affect Crouch in the weeks to come.

With the games continuing to come thick and fast, Europe appeared on the horizon once more as the Champions League group stages got under way. Liverpool had been grouped with Spaniards Real Betis, Anderlecht of Belgium and, remarkably, Premiership rivals Chelsea.

Under normal circumstances, teams from the same country cannot be drawn against each other but, as Liverpool had been forced to go through the qualification stages, they did not benefit from the usual same-country protection rules.

And their pairing with the men from Stamford Bridge immediately evoked memories of their controversial clash at the semi-final stage of the previous tournament just a few months earlier which had eventually been won by Liverpool thanks to a solitary goal over two legs by Luis Garcia – a goal that television pictures later seemed to prove had not crossed the line. Those matches would not be for the faint-hearted.

But first up was Real Betis and Liverpool made a dream start, racing into a two-goal lead after just 14 minutes courtesy of strikes from Florent Sinama Pongolle and Luis Garcia, and then protecting that advantage sufficiently to come away with a well-earned 2–1 victory.

But, while the goals continued to flow in Europe – the pair against Betis making it 19 in eight matches against foreign opposition already in various competitions, albeit against varying quality of opponents – it was the opposite story in the Premiership.

And when the next match, at home to arch-rivals Manchester United, also saw Liverpool draw a blank in another 0–0 stalemate, it meant the club had failed to score in three of their first four Premiership matches. They had found the net just once and had picked up just six points from a possible 12, hardly the flying start

Benitez would have wanted as he set about putting pressure on Chelsea, who had taken maximum points from their first four games.

Typically, he refused to panic, insisting in his post-match press conference, 'We lost to United twice last season, whereas this season we drew and controlled the game. We can't waste time worrying about the gap [with Chelsea].'

Another draw, this time away at Birmingham, did little to lift the gloom that was starting to descend over Anfield, although at least Liverpool fans had a couple of goals to cheer, with the game finishing 2–2. Crouch, however, had still not been able to break his duck.

By now, the gap to Chelsea was starting to grow and the pressure on Liverpool was starting to mount, and so it was typical of the footballing gods and their renowned sense of occasion in these circumstances that a glance at the fixture calendar by Reds fans would tell them that the next two matches pitted their side against the Premiership champions – firstly in the Champions League, followed just four days later by a domestic dust-up.

Both games would be played at Anfield, but they would have very different outcomes, as if to emphasise the alternate faces of Liverpool Football Club as displayed to British and foreign audiences, something that had been so evident in the previous campaign when their European glories stood in stark contrast to their home-grown woes.

In the Champions League, Liverpool fought and harried and generally enjoyed the best of the play against their London rivals, although their failings in front of goal still continued to undermine the good work being done in other areas of the pitch. As it was, however, a 0–0 draw to add to their victory in Betis meant four points and a solid start.

Given that most managers aim for ten points in the group stage to guarantee progress, Liverpool were well on their way to the knockout phase of the competition with four games left to play, particularly as the next two would see them play home and away ties against Anderlecht, widely perceived as being the weakest team in the group.

But any encouragement taken from that European draw against Chelsea was stripped bare when the two sides met again barely 90 hours later at the same venue. On this occasion, Liverpool were annihilated.

Goals from Frank Lampard, Damien Duff, Joe Cole and Geremi earned Chelsea a crushing 4–1 victory, with Liverpool having only Gerrard's first-half strike to show for their efforts. In the circumstances, it could hardly be called a consolation.

It may have been Liverpool's heaviest home defeat for 36 years, but Benitez insisted that his side had not deserved such a fate. After the match he said, 'We were in control but then made mistakes for all the goals. Chelsea didn't play any differently to the way they played last week [in the Champions League].

'They just drop and play on the counter-attack and whatever statistics you give me it's still the same – they play on the mistakes of other teams. We played to try and win the game.

'But we must not think about this game and the score. It was just one game. I don't want to think about Chelsea. I just think about my team. It was almost incredible that we could lose a game like that.'

But, for all Benitez's defiant words, it was clear to all onlookers that Liverpool were still some way short of challenging Chelsea's domestic dominance. On that night, the Reds had been punished for rare defensive sloppiness, but it was becoming abundantly clear that their real problems lay at the other end of the pitch.

They had scored just four goals in their first six Premiership matches, and only one of those had come from a striker – Cisse against Birmingham. And that had come from the penalty spot!

The Frenchman also scored in the next two matches to earn single-goal victories against Blackburn in the Premiership and Anderlecht in the Champions League as, in stark contrast to their faltering league form, the Reds continued their serene progress in that competition.

Benitez was trying everything to solve his side's goal-scoring problems. Different combinations were tried up front, different formations, sometimes with a lone striker and sometimes with two up front, but nothing seemed to be working. And poor Crouch, it seemed, could not buy a goal.

Another league defeat, this time by Fulham (2–0), was swiftly followed by an embarrassing League Cup exit at the hands of Championship side Crystal Palace (2–1) and what had merely been seen as a minor drama was in danger of turning into a full-blown crisis.

But, as so often happens in football, one victory would turn the whole season around. And that victory duly arrived in the next home match against West Ham. Liverpool beat the Hammers 2–0 at Anfield with goals from Xabi Alonso and Bolo Zenden; the result heralded the start of an 11-match unbeaten run in which, incredibly, they did not concede a single goal.

But, while the team's fortunes were about to take an upward turn, there was still no end in sight to Crouch's misery; as his side started to rack up the points, the new signing continued his fruitless search for his first goal in Liverpool colours.

By now, the critics were growing louder and more vociferous, although significantly none of the dissenting voices was coming from within the walls of Anfield. They, as you would expect, closed ranks around their under-fire colleague and continued to insist that he was playing well and working hard for the team. Publicly, they remained confident that the goals would come and, if there were any private doubts, they were kept firmly hidden.

Another win over Anderlecht – this time a convincing 3–0 victory at Anfield – took Liverpool to the brink of qualification for the knockout phase of the Champions League. The game almost provided a momentous moment for Crouch – in the shape of his first Reds goal – but, as he tried to pounce on the rebound following Silvio Proto's save from Morientes, he was just unable to hook his long leg around the ball and steer it towards goal. The agony would go on.

Another confident win, 2–0 away at Aston Villa, continued the team's progress but, against one of his former clubs, Crouch had to be content with a place on the bench and was unable to find the target in the 22 minutes he had on the pitch after coming on as a replacement for Morientes.

That marked his 14th game for the club – 11 starts and three substitute appearances – and still he awaited his first goal. Ironically, the next visitors to Anfield were Portsmouth, the club where he had enjoyed his most prolific spell, scoring at a rate of almost a goal every two games in his one season at Fratton Park. Perhaps the gods would smile on him at last?

On the eve of that match, he admitted he might get just a little carried away if he finally ended his drought against his former team.

He told the national media before that game, 'I'm really looking forward to the moment I score – and the sooner it comes the better. How will I celebrate? I think I'll want to jump into the Kop!

'There's been a lot said about me lately, but plenty of people have supported me as well. The manager here, the England coach Sven-Goran Eriksson, Wayne Rooney and Kenny Dalglish have all said nice things. When you hear positive comments from people you respect, it makes it easier to ignore the other stuff.

'And the Liverpool fans have been great with me. Everyone knows how loud they are and it's an amazing experience when they're singing your name. Hopefully I can get a goal for them this weekend.'

Crouch also received a vote of confidence from another under-fire striker, his team-mate Morientes, who had also found life tough in the Premiership. Indeed, his only three goals at this stage of the season had all come in the Champions League.

But the Spaniard was backing his strike partner to come good, insisting that there was more to Crouch's game than just goals. He told journalists, 'I enjoy playing next to Peter Crouch. He's very tall, he's strong and is very dangerous. When he is on form, he can cause a lot of pain for opposition defences with the problems he gives them. Maybe he is more of a provider than a 20-goals-a-season man. He still has the qualities needed to be a regular goalscorer, but we cannot ignore the way he provides assists for other players to score. He is an unselfish striker.'

Manager Benitez, meanwhile, urged Crouch to get tough as he sought his first goal against Portsmouth. He told the *Liverpool Daily Post*, 'Centre-forwards in England cannot be too nice – you must be aggressive and be hard against defenders, because they will be hard against you.

'He is a player with ability, but because he has quality does not mean he has to be so nice. For me it is important for him to improve in such areas, he is a very good lad, but maybe too nice. It is difficult to change these things, but he is clever and he can see what he needs to do.

'Peter has a knack of changing games, we are aware he can do that and we know he can give us another style and way of playing. He is different to the others and he is well liked and respected, and that is why lots of people in our dressing room and England's understand and appreciate what he does.

'I know he has said he will jump into the Kop when he scores, but I always say to him that if he gives the team something different and always works hard that is enough; I do not care who scores the goals.

'If his team-mates can score goals, I will be happy. He creates a lot of space when he comes on, he creates chaos sometimes and real problems.'

But Crouch was only too well aware that, for all the kind words from his fellow players for both club and country, and for the votes of confidence from both his club and international manager, strikers are judged on goals. And he needed to start scoring.

And so he couldn't have wished for a better opportunity than the one that arrived after 22 minutes against Portsmouth when referee Peter Walton awarded Liverpool a penalty. And, after a consultation with Gerrard and Cisse, it was Crouch who put the ball on the spot.

Sadly, however, and perhaps typically given the way his luck was going, his spot-kick was saved by Jamie Ashdown. His misery was shared by the vast majority of the 44,000 crowd at Anfield. It was another huge blow to his confidence.

Fortunately for Liverpool, though, the damage was not too serious. The rebound from Crouch's penalty fell perfectly for Zenden to head the team into the lead, and they made sure of the three points with further goals from Cisse and Morientes – the Spaniard's first Premiership goal of the season, of course, and one which was set up by Crouch; it proved that the front man was not ready to give up the fight just yet.

But, while his fellow attackers were celebrating, Crouch was left to reflect on what had been another disheartening missed opportunity. He told the media afterwards, 'I wasn't going to hide when the penalty was given. That's one thing I will never do and I made the decision about who was going to take it. I have taken quite a few before and scored one against Portsmouth [for Southampton] in the final minute last season, so I was confident. I changed my mind at the last moment about which side to put it, but that's how it goes sometimes.

'I am desperate to score my first Liverpool goal and, if we get another penalty, I'll be the first to put my hand up. I get the feeling the fans are willing me to score, because they know I'm doing my best.'

Manager Benitez echoed those sentiments and agreed that the fans were desperate to see Crouch finally get his name on the scoresheet. He said in his post-match press conference, 'Always, when he has a chance near goal, he can hear the fans cheering him and willing him to score. Maybe they want him to score too much. You can understand how they feel, but it can increase the levels of anxiety a bit.

'If you analyse his performances, he is doing everything right. You cannot fault him and he has the full support of his team-mates, as well as the crowd. They are desperate for him to score. It will happen. And, when he gets one, he will get a lot more.'

Liverpool continued to win, claiming successive away victories at Manchester City and Sunderland, and also drawing 0–0 at home to Real Betis to confirm their place in the knockout phase of the Champions League – the least they deserved for their efforts, having been forced to enter the competition in the first qualifying round way back in July.

Crouch's debut, of course, had come in the first leg of the second qualifying round against FBK Kaunas on 26 July. Now, as the calendar moved into December, he had played 21 matches – 18 for Liverpool and three for England – without a goal. The pressure was building.

By now, bookies were taking bets on the misfiring forward to go the entire season without scoring a goal. Bet365 were offering odds of 12/1 on that happening and spokesman Steve Freeth said at the time, 'Punters have piled on [the money]. We'll be more relieved than him if he scores – we've laid him at 20/1, 16/1 and 14/1 not to find the net!'

Next up, in Crouch's 19th match for Liverpool, were Premiership new boys Wigan, making their first appearance at Anfield for 17 years. Could this be the day when Crouch's prayers were answered and when that elusive goal finally arrived? After more than 24 hours of playing time, would this be the day when the jokes about the striker who can play all day without scoring would finally end?

After 19 minutes, the world got its answer. Or did it?

Crouch's 25-yard shot deflected off defender Leighton Baines and flew into the air, arcing over goalkeeper Mike Pollitt who, in frantically trying to claw the ball over the crossbar, only succeeded in helping it on its way over the goal-line. Was it Crouch's goal or an own goal?

The noise level inside Anfield left no one in any doubt as 40,000 home fans rose to cheer and applaud. And Crouch's 70-yard sprint of celebration down the touchline was evidence that he was certainly going to claim it. You had the feeling that it would take a brave man to try to take it off him!

He told reporters after the match, 'Of course I am claiming it. It was on target and if you start ruling an own goal every time a goalkeeper gets a hand to the ball and it goes over the line there will be precious few goals awarded to strikers.'

Benitez added, 'He was shooting for goal, it was on target and it doesn't matter who touched it. The goal is Peter's.'

In the end, though, the arguments over that strike didn't really matter all that much because, three minutes before half-time, he got another one – and there was no doubt about whose goal it was this time – finishing as he did with an exquisite lob over the advancing Pollitt that gave the goalkeeper absolutely no chance.

Luis Garcia added a third 20 minutes from the end of the match to round off a good day for Liverpool, and a fantastic one for Crouch.

He continued, 'I have been worried, I have taken a lot of stick, and I just wanted it to end with a goal. But everyone at the club has been so supportive, the manager has always said I am playing well, and we are winning. And that is all that mattered.

Everyone around Liverpool has been great with me. My team-mates, manager and the fans have been top class. It is much easier when the people who matter believe in you. Other clubs may not have been so patient. Fans would have had a go at me, but there's been nothing like that here.

'The fans have been willing me on and the goals are for them as well as for me. I cannot speak highly enough of the supporters. There are others who have their own opinions, but maybe they are not watching the amount of games our fans do.

'But I also believe in myself and I believe I can go on a little run now. The manager has never had any problems. He has always said just keep doing what you are doing. I am a buoyant person by nature, but if I'm honest this goal drought has been getting me down at times. I've been getting a bit of stick lately, but it's great to get the goals and hopefully I can go on from here and score more.

'I am lucky because there are an awful lot of people who have believed in me. When I have gone through a barren spell they have buoyed me up and I am sure that over the next few days people will be texting me and phoning me and I need to thank those people for keeping me going.

'I really, really wanted to score. I am pleased for myself, but I am also pleased for the team. The lads at the back have done very well, especially Carra [Jamie Carragher] and Sami [Sami Hyypia] – we have been keeping clean sheets and defending well throughout the side. We have to keep that run going now.

'It was a good team performance and great to get the three points today. We are up to second now and playing well. The defence has kept another clean sheet and that makes our life easier up front. All of this gives us confidence and bodes well for the future.'

Benitez, who had said in the build-up to the game that he didn't care if Crouch didn't score all season as long as he continued to play well and contributed to the team effort, reiterated his point after the match.

He told the media, 'Peter will score goals. He has scored them everywhere he has been and he will score them for Liverpool. But I don't really mind whether he scores them or not. If Jamie Carragher gets them and Peter doesn't, then I will be happy.

'The way we play, we need someone to hold the ball up for us, to give us time to get up in support and play football around the penalty area. Peter gives us the chance to do that. There is nobody better at holding the ball up, at giving us the time to support, and when we get there we create the chances for a lot of players to score, not just the strikers.

'Look at our record when Peter was not scoring. We won all the games and we didn't concede a goal. We were winning, and he was contributing to our victories. So, when I said I was happy, I was.'

Liverpool's fine form continued as they again drew 0–0 with Chelsea in their second meeting of the season in the Champions League – and their third overall – this time at Stamford Bridge. And having lost 4–1 at home in the Premiership to the same opponents just a couple of months earlier, it demonstrated the progress Liverpool had made.

It was also further evidence that Liverpool appear to be a different team when they face Chelsea in cup competitions rather than in a league environment, even though this game was the culmination of a mini-league of its own. The result ensured that the Reds remained unbeaten throughout the first phase and topped the group, meaning they would avoid the other group winners in the second stage.

A routine Premiership victory over Middlesbrough followed, meaning that Liverpool were in high spirits and excellent form as they jetted to Japan to take part in the Club World Championship.

Their first match – indeed their semi-final – was against Deportivo Saprissa of Costa Rica, and after Crouch had given them a third-minute lead the outcome was never in doubt. Gerrard added a second before

Crouch grabbed a third to make it 3–0 and ensure a smooth passage into the final, where they would meet the Brazilian side Sao Paolo.

The clean sheet kept by goalkeeper Reina in that match was the side's 11th in a row, a new club record, beating the mark set by the title-winning side of 1987–88, and Benitez was delighted that his side had earned themselves a place in the club's record books.

He told the media, 'We wanted to keep a clean sheet, our 11th in a row. It was the same against Middlesbrough the other day – Pepe Reina made some good saves and the defenders and the whole team have worked hard. They deserve to go down in history, and the history of a big club is always important.'

And Crouch was thrilled to have reached his first final with Liverpool. He told reporters after the game, 'Reaching the final is a special moment for me, because it gives me the chance to play in a major game with a major prize. I won a Championship medal with Norwich when I just squeaked in with about 12 games on loan when they won the title and were promoted, but I wasn't really part of that.

'I honestly can't remember the last time I won a medal. It could even have been a tennis one, I'm not so sure. But that's why I came to Liverpool, to compete at the top and give myself the chance of winning honours. If we win this, we'll be the world champions, and that means a lot.

'It's a special time at the moment. I know it took a while to get off the mark, but I always knew it would come, and I was confident and happy out there. I enjoyed those two goals, especially the first.

'I hit it really sweetly and I knew it was in as soon as it left my foot. Now it's Sao Paulo in the final – another great game to be involved in, and one we know we can win.'

The history books, however, would not record a Club World Championship success for Liverpool, nor would their defensive record stretch to 12 matches, as they were beaten 1–0 by the Brazilians, courtesy of a 28th-minute winner from Mineiro.

But the Reds were furious at the standard of officiating, after having three goals ruled out by the same Canadian linesman. Television pictures suggested that Hector Vergara was correct with his first two decisions to disallow goals from Luis Garcia and Sami Hyypia, but there was little doubt that Florent Sinama Pongolle's 89th-minute effort should have counted.

Benitez made an official complaint to FIFA president Sepp Blatter about the standard of refereeing in the final, and he admitted, 'I try to respect the opposition because they're a good team. But the stats show we have had 21 shots, 17 corners, hit the crossbar twice and scored three goals.

'And it was unbelievable the referee didn't show a red card for a foul on Steven Gerrard. The centre-back has fouled Stevie, who was running with the ball. The rules say, if you can't play the ball and foul the player, it is a red card. I don't understand these things.

'I can't understand why only three minutes were added on when there had been a lot of stoppages in the game. I talked to the officials at the end of the game, but you can't change things. But something should change if you want to give importance to this competition. To play just one game before the final, and to not water the pitch, is not the most common thing.

'And you wouldn't get a Mexican referee and a Canadian linesman in the final of the World Cup. They replayed a lot of instances on the big screen [in the stadium], but not the goal – why? Everyone has seen we've scored three goals.

'I am disappointed with how the situation was controlled by the referee. I really think we deserved to win.'

Luis Garcia was even more vitriolic, insisting that Liverpool felt 'cheated'. He fumed to reporters afterwards, 'We feel cheated. They tell me it wasn't a goal, but what can you do now? We can't do anything.

'We scored three and one was definitely a goal. I think the referee was clearly wrong with some of his decisions and we are really unhappy about it. We have lost out on the trophy, but we know we've played well. They had one chance, and nothing else after that.

'At least I think we showed everyone that we can compete with the best teams in the world, and I believe we can kick on from this now.'

So Liverpool returned home from Japan empty-handed, but crucially the trip did not appear to have disturbed their rhythm which had seen them in such irrepressible form in the build-up to the tournament.

They hit the ground running back in the Premiership as they set about consolidating their position in the top three. Newcastle were beaten 2–0 at Anfield on Boxing Day, with Crouch netting his third goal in his last three Premiership matches, to add to the two he scored in

Japan. The man who seemed to have forgotten how to find the back of the net simply couldn't stop scoring.

Two days later, the Reds made the short trip across Stanley Park to face Everton and came away 3–1 winners in a match that saw the home side reduced to nine men following the sendings-off of Mikel Arteta and Phil Neville.

But by the time the pair were dismissed – Neville in the 68th minute and Arteta in the 90th – Liverpool were already 3–1 up, courtesy of goals from Crouch, his first in a Merseyside derby, Gerrard and Cisse.

It was Liverpool's ninth league win in a row, their best run since 1989, and Benitez was delighted. He said afterwards, 'We knew what we had to do. We knew it would be a physical game, and we tried to control the game. We knew they would make mistakes and we had to be ready for them.

'We wanted to start with a high tempo because we thought we could get opportunities. It was just a question of time. I am very happy with the win, but we did not play to our level. We played the game as we needed to play, but I think we have played better games, such as away against Aston Villa.

'For 15 to 20 minutes in the first half, we were losing the second balls and came under pressure. But overall I think the team played well. We are playing with a lot of confidence.'

The Spaniard also had a special word of praise for Crouch, who made it four goals in four games in the league. He added, 'Peter Crouch is playing well. He is now scoring goals too, and I am happy for him. The most important thing for me is that he is still playing well, but if we continue winning then I won't mind how many he scores.

'We were thinking about using two different kinds of players up front. Crouch can win balls in the air and keep the ball, while Cisse can run. We knew they would be a little bit nervous and would defend high and leave space behind, and that's why we went with him. Cisse is the kind of player you can use when the other team is going forward and playing a high line in defence.

'The team has the confidence we need and the strikers are now scoring goals. We are creating more chances and the strikers are more confident. The big difference with last season is that this season we can use the likes of Sissoko and Crouch and we have different players we can play should we want to play the long game, the short game or a more physical game.'

Despite their great run, however, Liverpool still trailed leaders Chelsea by a massive 15 points as the turn of the year approached. Not that anyone at Anfield was ready to throw in the title towel just yet.

After the Everton victory, Liverpool captain Gerrard insisted, 'We'll keep going, trying to make up ground. If Manchester United and Chelsea drop points, then we want to make sure we can take advantage. Chelsea aren't dropping many points, but we've just got to concentrate on what we're doing.'

The final game of the year saw Liverpool make it ten Premiership wins in a row, and also provided a fitting climax for Crouch as he netted the only goal of the game at Anfield to defeat West Bromwich Albion.

And what a year 2005 had been!

From the lows of relegation with Southampton to an England debut and a £7 million move to Liverpool, and all the trials and tribulations that accompanied his first few months at Anfield as he simply couldn't find a way to end his goal drought, it had been an incredible 12 months for the big striker. Not bad for a player ditched for just £2 million by Aston Villa only 18 months previously!

And he was given a further boost when Gerrard slammed the critics who had written off Crouch during his early days at Anfield. Talking after the striker had netted the winner against West Brom, Gerrard told the ranks of assembled media, 'Peter has been superb for us since the first day he came. He was playing really well even when he wasn't scoring; he was doing well for the team and I wonder where all the critics are now who were on his back.

'They are probably hiding or just shaking their heads as they watch him now; they are no doubt asking themselves why they said what they did. It was only a matter of time before he scored.

'He is proving to everyone that he is England class and I'm sure he has a bright international future. I certainly hope he has.'

It was a ringing endorsement of Crouch's qualities and further proof that his team-mates appreciated the work he did, even if the sceptics still struggled to see beyond his ungainly appearance.

Liverpool's phenomenal run of victories finally came to an end in the first game of 2006 when they were held to a 2–2 draw at Bolton, before their next away trip – to face

Luton in an FA Cup third-round tie – produced one of the most astonishing games the famous old competition has ever witnessed.

After Gerrard had given the visitors the lead in the 16th minute, Luton raced into a 3–1 lead thanks to goals from Steve Howard, Steve Robinson and Kevin Nicholls to leave the European champions wobbling and on the brink of a huge upset.

But, in an astonishing turnaround and in a demonstration of stunning attacking football, the Reds bounced back to win by 5–3 with Sinama Pongolle and Xabi Alonso netting twice each, the second from the Spaniard, in the very last minute, coming from inside his own half after Luton goalkeeper Marlon Beresford had gone forward for a corner.

It was an extraordinary ending to an extraordinary match, and evoked memories of that night in Istanbul eight months earlier when Liverpool had staged that remarkable recovery to win the European Cup. Although, to be fair, even the most ardent Luton fan would admit that their side is no AC Milan!

For Benitez, though, the memories were not necessarily happy ones. 'I don't like those comebacks very much,' he told the press corps. 'It is not good for my heart. After scoring the first goal, we thought it would be easy, but then we gave them a lot of opportunities.

'At the end, the most important thing was that we went through – but we have to learn that when we are the better team we need to finish the game off. I was unhappy with the way we played in the first half. We had big problems when we conceded our third goal, but I still had confidence in my team. It was difficult for us because Luton played a fantastic game.'

A 1–0 home win over Tottenham followed as Liverpool extended their incredible run of unbeaten matches against domestic opponents to 14, including the games against Chelsea in the Champions League, with the only blot on their copybook being that controversial defeat to Sao Paulo in Japan.

That run stretched from 29 October 2005 until 22 January 2006 when it was ended at Old Trafford, of all places, against Manchester United. In a game Liverpool dominated, they were devastated to find themselves on the wrong end of a 1–0 scoreline, courtesy of Rio Ferdinand's last-minute header.

It was a cruel blow for Liverpool and, although Benitez was incensed by referee Mike Riley's decision to award the crucial free-kick from which Ferdinand scored – when Steve Finnan was adjudged to have fouled Patrice Evra – he knew that ultimately his side had only themselves to blame for a string of missed chances, the worst of which saw Cisse blaze over from six yards out when faced with an open goal.

After the game, Benitez said, 'That is maybe the most disappointed I have been this season. We were controlling the game in the second half and we had done a good job in keeping the ball and playing good counter-attacks.

'So to concede a goal in the last minute from a free-kick is not normal. Now we need to think about what we can change. We had made some good counter-attacks, but we need to finish [our chances]. We controlled the game for most of the time against a good team.

'You cannot say congratulations to the players because we lost, but we have done a very good job. But if you concede in the last minute then you have made a mistake. We have done all the right things for at least not losing the game. But always the small details can make the difference.'

Liverpool put that defeat behind them as they advanced into the fifth round of the FA Cup with a 2–1 win at the home of Crouch's old club, Portsmouth, but the Old Trafford loss was perhaps still on the players' minds as they suffered a crucial mid-season blip in the Premiership.

Following that setback against their great rivals, they could only draw their next Premiership match – at home to struggling Birmingham – and then lost twice within three days in London, firstly to Chelsea and then to Charlton.

The defeat to Chelsea was a particularly bitter pill to swallow and offered further evidence as to Liverpool's curious failures against the men from Stamford Bridge in league competition, when placed alongside their record against them in cup tournaments.

And there was further anger and recrimination emanating from the Liverpool camp after goalkeeper Reina was sent off eight minutes from time after clashing with Arjen Robben. Referee Alan Wiley was about to book Reina for a poor challenge on Eidur Gudjohnsen near the touchline, when Robben chose to intervene.

Reina pushed his gloved hand into the Dutchman's face and Robben collapsed to the ground in a heap and the goalkeeper's expected yellow card was switched immediately for a red one.

Benitez could scarcely conceal his anger afterwards. He raged sarcastically to reporters after the game, 'I am in a hurry as I must go the hospital. Robben must be in there because the injury was so serious.

'Let me be clear, Reina has made a mistake by allowing Robben to provoke him and turning around and touching his face. He does not need to do that, but you can see from the television that maybe Robben will be in hospital for three weeks with a broken neck.

'The referee must see the situation. Nothing happened really. I have not spoken to the referee, but I spoke to the fourth official and said I was surprised by the decision. I don't understand how these things work. You can kick a player all game and maybe only get a yellow card, but you then touch another in the face and you are banned for three games.

'Maybe Reina should have fallen over when Gallas touched him in the face just after that.'

The defeat left Liverpool six points behind Manchester United in second place, and a massive 21 points adrift of Chelsea. It also extended the club's wretched run at Stamford Bridge to just one win in 19 matches.

But the visitors had their chances, particularly in the first half, as Benitez made clear. 'We created chances in the first half and controlled a lot of things,' he continued. 'But we made a mistake at a corner and then Chelsea could play the way they like to play, on the counter-attack. The chances they had in the second half were because we were pressing forward.

'It is true that we need to score more goals, as we are creating chances and the statistics are good in attack. I was happy with how we played in the first half. But if you make mistakes against the big teams, then it is going to be difficult.'

Any hopes Liverpool may have had of somehow hauling themselves back into the title race were clearly over, leaving them with only the Champions League and the FA Cup still to play for.

And so, less then a month after Manchester United had ended their unbeaten streak and knocked them out of their stride in the Premiership, the two sides lined up against one another in their FA Cup fifth-round tie at Anfield.

The game may have been overshadowed by the horror injury sustained by Alan Smith that saw him break his leg and dislocate his ankle joint, but, while there was huge sympathy for Smith from within the Liverpool camp, there was no escaping the joy they felt at knocking out United courtesy of a solitary first-half goal from Crouch. His towering header hit the foot of the post and rolled behind goalkeeper Edwin van der Sar and into the net.

It was Crouch's first goal in nine games, and the first by any Liverpool striker in 2006. And he was delighted with it, telling the club's website, 'Liverpool against Man United is probably the biggest fixture in English football and so to get the winner was certainly something special, especially after the way our hearts were broken against them in the last minute at Old Trafford.

'I think beating them in the FA Cup makes up for that. It was a deserved victory; we competed with them, played at a high tempo and probably created the better chances.

It was an enjoyable win and the fact it meant so much to the fans makes it even more special.'

Despite that goal, though, Crouch was aware that the pressure was starting to build once more on the Liverpool strike-force, particularly with the return to the club of former hero Robbie Fowler during the January transfer window a couple of weeks earlier.

He continued in the same interview: 'A striker's main job is to score goals and, obviously, we all want to be hitting the back of the net on a regular basis. But, as long as we are scoring goals as a team, then there isn't much of a problem. Obviously, Robbie's come in now and competition for places is more intense. Because of his signing, all the strikers will have to play well and start scoring to stay in the team.'

But, while there was joy in the FA Cup, there was misery in the Champions League as Liverpool's defence of the trophy ended in bitterly disappointing fashion. Having worked so hard to top their group and therefore avoid the big guns in the first knockout phase, they would have been delighted to have been paired with Benfica, a team widely accepted to be one of the weakest, and possibly even the weakest, left in the tournament.

And having performed creditably in the first leg in Portugal, losing only by one goal to nil, Liverpool would have been confident of overhauling that deficit and finishing the job off in front of their own fans. Instead, they slumped to a hugely disappointing 2–0 defeat on one of the most miserable European nights ever witnessed at Anfield.

It was a thoroughly unsatisfactory end to their reign as European champions and once more the finger of blame was being pointed at the club's strikers. After just four goals in their last nine matches, it was clear that Liverpool's early-season problems of finding the back of the net had surfaced again at the worst possible time.

Not that Benitez was keen to lay the blame entirely at the feet of his front-line attackers. He told the media at Anfield that night, 'If you create chances and can't score goals, maybe you need to create more chances. It's not just about strikers. It's about defence as well and controlling the midfield.

'It was clear that we had enough chances to win the game. But we made a mistake and conceded a goal. In the second half, we were looking for an early goal, but we had the same problem and couldn't score. For me, the problem is that we conceded that second goal.

'But I will not blame my strikers. Mistakes were made at the back and that is why we lost. I am really, really disappointed. We had a lot of confidence. You could see on the faces of the players before the game we believed it was possible. But we did not play well and we did not play at our level.'

Skipper Gerrard was equally disappointed, and shared his manager's frustrations that opportunities to score were simply not being taken. He told reporters clamouring for quotes in the post-match mixed zone, 'I am disappointed we didn't take our chances. We are creating chances but have a lack of goals at the moment and we need to work on it.

'We were the much better team but could not put any of those chances away. But good luck to Benfica. It was important to get an early goal. We created three good early chances but did not put them away and when Benfica scored you began to worry.

'We will have to have extra shooting sessions in training. We know we have the personnel to score those goals. Now we need to pick ourselves up. The FA Cup becomes even more important now; we need a trophy.'

But a further Premiership defeat followed at Arsenal, and there was a danger that a promising season would drift away and end in disappointment, with the club trophyless. They certainly needed a lift from somewhere.

And when you need a lift, who better to come calling than a team that had failed to win a single Premiership match away from home all season? And so every Liverpool fan would have been delighted to see the name of Fulham next on the club's fixture list.

And, as if on cue, the Londoners arrived at Anfield and were promptly hammered 5–1 as Liverpool finally rediscovered their goal touch.

It was always going to be a good night for the home fans once Fowler had scored his first goal since his return to the club from Manchester City and, even though Collins John levelled for the visitors after 25 minutes, the goal merely delayed the inevitable.

A Michael Brown own goal restored Liverpool's lead before the break, and three further goals in the final 20 minutes – from Morientes, Crouch and Stephen Warnock – made sure that everyone went home happy.

That win kept Liverpool firmly in control of third place in the table and rounded off a perfect day for the club, after it had earlier been revealed that Benitez had agreed a new four-year contract.

His agent had spent the afternoon of the match in talks with chief executive Rick Parry and the Spaniard said, 'We are talking and the relationship with the fans is fantastic. I'm happy, they're happy and it's not a problem.'

On the victory over Fulham, he added, 'It was a fantastic game for the strikers. As a manager, to see all the forwards scoring or involved in the goals is great. They knew they needed to score. I hope now that will give them confidence for the rest of the season.'

And just four days later, when the team took to the field again against Newcastle, that certainly looked to be the case. They ran out confident 3–1 winners at St James' Park, with Crouch putting them on their way with a tenth-minute opener.

Further goals from Gerrard and a Cisse penalty rendered Shola Amoebi's 41st-minute strike irrelevant and ensured that Liverpool's assault on the top three continued.

Newcastle ended the game with ten men after defender Jean-Alain Boumsong was dismissed for a foul on Crouch, but Benitez insisted that the red card had done nothing to affect the outcome of the game, and he was delighted with his side's display.

After the match he said, 'The sending-off was not too important because the team was winning when it was 11 against 11. We were creating chances and playing well, so it wasn't as if it was a turning point.

'As supporters, our fans must be delighted. If you want to win titles you need a good squad. We played a new system and I'm pleased with the way the team adapted. They proved they are good players.'

And the Anfield boss was equally pleased to see both of

his strikers – Crouch and Cisse – on the scoresheet again, as the forwards' poor run of form in front of goal seemed to have become a distant memory.

He added, 'It is really important for the team to see the strikers scoring goals and it has given me a good problem for the next game. They will have more confidence for the coming games. Peter Crouch showed why we signed him as he scored a good goal, kept the ball and won headers. For the English league it's very important to have a player like him.

'It was important to win and our idea is the same and that is to win one game at a time, to keep going and keep closing the gap on Manchester United. It's important to finish second and if we continue to win games it's still possible.'

But while Benitez was happy to see his side continue their winning run, he was less pleased with the Football Association and with the fixture pile-up that saw his team facing a crucial FA Cup quarter-final against Birmingham just two days after playing Newcastle.

He insisted, 'It's crazy that we have another game in two days and I don't understand it, but it's a very important game against Birmingham in the FA Cup and that it why it is so important to have a good squad.

'The thing I don't understand is you must play with your strongest team, but my strongest team will all be tired.'

Benitez went into the game at St Andrew's keen to put right a record that had seen his side fail to beat Birmingham since his arrival in England. He added, 'I haven't beaten them yet as Liverpool manager, but I hope to change that.

'We controlled both games against Birmingham in the

Premiership this season but scored own goals in both. Maybe I need to say to the players don't stand too close to Reina!

'We have confidence and the strikers are scoring goals again which I hope to see continue until the end of the season.'

As it was, however, the Spaniard needn't have had any worries, either about his players showing signs of fatigue after their punishing schedule, or of his hoodoo continuing against Birmingham.

However, not even the most optimistic of Liverpool fans could have expected that the Reds would put that record straight quite so emphatically. But, from the moment Hyypia took advantage of some slack Birmingham defending in the very first minute, it was clear that this was going to be a night for Liverpool to enjoy, and for the Blues' fans to endure.

Crouch made it 2–0 after only five minutes as Liverpool continued their electrifying start, and he added a third before half-time to kill off the game as a contest completely.

Birmingham's only hope, with a potential place in the semi-finals wiped out inside 45 minutes, was that they would be able to stem the tide after the interval and avoid humiliation. Sadly for them, they were unable to do so.

Morientes made it four after 59 minutes, and Riise added a fifth 11 minutes later. Oliver Tebily then compounded the hosts' misery with a 77th-minute own goal, before Cisse completed the rout with a seventh goal a minute before the end of normal time.

As bad as Birmingham had been on the night, though, it had nonetheless been an extraordinary performance by

Liverpool in their third game in a week, and their sixth in just 21 days. It was also Liverpool's best ever win away from Anfield in the FA Cup, and the biggest victory in the quarter-finals of the competition since 1890.

But, while the team was thrilled with the victory and a place in the last four of the competition, there was a tinge of disappointment for Crouch, who had been substituted for Morientes 11 minutes into the second half.

He admitted to the media afterwards, 'I was a bit gutted not to have a chance of a hat-trick. But I think the manager was thinking about the Everton game. It was a great performance by us and a good result. It's always the case that when you score a couple of goals then the next ones tend to go in a bit easier. Hopefully, we can keep this run going now.'

The Everton game he referred to was Liverpool's next Premiership encounter as the matches continued to come thick and fast. And having already beaten their Mersey rivals 3–1 at Goodison Park in December, the red half of the city was determined to complete the double over their old foes.

Captain Gerrard told the local press on the eve of the match, 'I was listening to some of the Everton players saying they were happy to be coming to Anfield full of confidence, but I think it's the same for us now.

'We've been getting criticised for not scoring goals of late, but hopefully we have proved the critics wrong. We were really pleased with our performance against Birmingham.

'Nothing has changed in terms of why we're suddenly scoring goals. I just think we're getting more luck now. We've always been playing well, but the strikers hadn't been having much luck. Now they're starting to go in and we're delighted.'

For Gerrard, though, the derby would prove a bitter-sweet affair. The Anfield midfield ace found himself right at the heart of the action in the opening quarter, but for all the wrong reasons. And his match lasted just 18 minutes before referee Phil Dowd brandished two yellow cards in his direction within 60 seconds, firstly for kicking the ball away and then for chopping down Kevin Kilbane. He was forced to watch the rest of the game as a frustrated fan as his team battled on with ten men.

Remarkably though, despite being deprived of their inspirational main man, Liverpool ran out 3–1 winners. Phil Neville put through his own goal on the stroke of half-time and, just two minutes after the restart, Luis Garcia gave the home side some breathing space with the second goal of the game.

Tim Cahill did pull one back for Everton just past the hour mark, but the visitors also found themselves a man down after 74 minutes when Andy van der Meyde was sent off after catching Alonso with his elbow as they tussled for the ball.

And the Blues' misery was completed six minutes from time when Harry Kewell wrapped up the points with superb 25-yard strike.

That meant joy tempered with relief for Benitez, but he issued stern words of warning to his side, and to his captain in particular. He said in his after-match press conference, 'We must learn, Steven and all the players, that you can play with the brain as well as the heart.

Steven gives us a lot of things, he plays with passion, but in this type of game you need to be calm.'

Gerrard himself was relieved that his team-mates had saved his embarrassment by winning the game without him. He told the press, 'The lads were all heroic – every one of them. I didn't want to get them in trouble, but they were brilliant. You wouldn't have known we had ten men for so long. I can't praise them enough and they certainly made me feel better about things at the end.'

That victory meant the Liverpool juggernaut continued to roll forward and they had now extended their winning run to four games, scoring 18 goals in the process and conceding just three. Little wonder then that confidence among the squad was sky high.

A routine victory over struggling West Brom came next, followed by two narrow battling 1–0 successes over north-west rivals Bolton and Blackburn. But those are the sort of games champion sides need to win, games where they have to fight against more limited opponents, and those are the kind of encounters previous Liverpool sides would have drawn or even lost.

But Benitez had instilled an iron will into his side that ensured that, even when the goals were not flowing, they were defensively solid and could eke out victories when the need arose.

They had now won their last seven games in all competitions, but next up was potentially their toughest test of the season so far – an FA Cup semi-final date with Chelsea, their fifth meeting of a remarkable season.

So far, Liverpool had failed to beat Jose Mourinho's side, losing both Premiership clashes and drawing their two Champions League games, but with a place in the FA Cup final at stake, only victory on this occasion would suffice.

And having beaten the Premiership champions over two legs the previous spring in a controversial Champions League semi-final, Liverpool knew they could do it. But, as they approached their ninth clash with the men from Stamford Bridge in just two years, they were taking nothing for granted.

Jamie Carragher admitted on the club's website, 'We realise it's going to be difficult and that we are going to be underdogs. We have played nine times and won only once, but that match was the most important of all. This will also be very important and hopefully we can win it again.

'We will have to keep it tight at the back, because they do the same. We are similar because we are both strong at the back. You cannot afford to waste any opportunities because there shouldn't be too many in the game. To beat Chelsea you are probably going to have to keep a clean sheet, that is what we are looking to do.'

With West Ham facing Middlesbrough in the other semi-final, Liverpool could have been handed an easier-looking task to get to the Millennium Stadium, but Carragher had no worries about playing Chelsea.

He added, 'To win the FA Cup we'd have to beat Chelsea anyway. If we had got one of the other teams, you'd expect Chelsea to be in the final. Everything you want to do now, you are going to have to beat Chelsea. To win the European Cup, we had to beat Chelsea.

'To win the FA Cup we'll have to beat Chelsea and to win the league you are going to have to beat them. As for all this stuff about hoping not to play them – just play them. You have to beat them to win things, that is the way it is.'

Carragher's defiant attitude certainly seemed to inspire those around him as Liverpool once again wrecked Mourinho's cup dreams. Just 12 months after knocking his side out at the final hurdle in Europe, they did so again at Old Trafford and ended any hopes Chelsea might have had of completing the domestic double.

Goals from Riise and Luis Garcia put the Reds 2–0 up, before Didier Drogba pulled one back for the champions elect. But, even though they had further chances, with Joe Cole squandering a particularly good opportunity in the dying moments of the game, it was Liverpool's day as they ran out 2–1 winners.

Not that there were to be any words of congratulation from Mourinho. The self-proclaimed 'Special One', who had protested long and hard about Garcia's decisive strike in the Champions League meeting 12 months previously, was in a similarly uncharitable mood.

He claimed that Liverpool should never have been awarded the free-kick from which Riise gave them the lead, and also insisted that John Terry's header in the first half, which would have made the scores level, should not have been disallowed.

But none of his gripes bothered Liverpool one bit. And Garcia was particularly pleased that his decisive strike had been a wonderful dipping 25-yard volley and not a close-range poke like the one that had prompted so much controversy during that Champions League semi-final, with Chelsea continuing to insist that the ball had been cleared off the line.

The little Spaniard told the press, 'There was no doubt that one was over the line! I was delighted with the finish and it was important.'

Benitez, too, was thrilled to be heading for the final. He said in his media conference, 'I am really happy and delighted for the players, the club and the supporters. It was an amazing game for us. The big clubs are always thinking about winning the big trophies and we are in the most famous cup final in the world. It is really important for us to win.'

Before they could think about the FA Cup final, however, there were three Premiership matches to play as they looked to overhaul Manchester United for second spot and automatic qualification for the Champions League.

However, by a curious twist of fate, their next match – just four days after that defeat of Chelsea – saw them travel south to East London to take on West Ham at Upton Park, in what would be a rehearsal for the final that was only 17 days away.

Liverpool collected the win they needed to move to within three points of United, thanks to a double from Cisse. He scored either side of Nigel Reo-Coker's goal for the home team to secure a 2–1 win, but there were to be repercussions for both sides ahead of that Cardiff date.

Luis Garcia and West Ham's Hayden Mullins were both sent off after clashing just eight minutes from time and, although both sides appealed the decision, the FA upheld their three-match bans and both players would miss the showpiece final at the Millennium Stadium.

Liverpool made it ten wins on the bounce by beating Aston Villa in their penultimate Premiership match of the season, meaning they could yet nick second spot from Manchester United if they beat Portsmouth on the final day and Sir Alex Ferguson's side failed to get the three points against Charlton.

And they were in confident mood as they approached their trip to the south coast, with Crouch in particular looking forward to the return to his old club.

He told the press ahead of the game, 'Second place is still possible, even if it did appear to be slipping away from us. We know Manchester United will have to slip up, but we will fight right to the end. We have put a good run together and want to finish the season strongly.

'And, whatever happens, we will be looking to take this form into next season. When you are at a club like this you have to keep improving. And we have improved this season; our league position and points tally underlines that. The manager said last season that, although we won the Champions League, he was disappointed with the league position and our form.

'We are third at the moment, aiming for second, but we are intent on going even higher next season.'

Liverpool did all that was asked of them at Fratton Park, winning 3–1, with Crouch netting Liverpool's second goal, sandwiched between efforts from Fowler and Cisse. But, ultimately, it marked a frustrating end to the campaign, as they fell just one point short of Manchester United, who thumped Charlton 4–0, in their quest for second spot.

Afterwards, Benitez was forced to admit that his side's lack of goals at crucial stages of the season was what cost them their place in the top two.

He told the media, 'The problem was that we started

playing well but we couldn't score the goals we needed. At this moment we are close to Chelsea. We feel we can do something next season. To get 82 points is fantastic, but maybe we need to win more against the bigger teams next season. We must be happy with the progress of the team, but we need to improve a little bit if we want to win the title.'

That appeared to be a pretty good summing up of Liverpool's league season but with one match still to play – the FA Cup final – Crouch could reflect on a successful first season at Anfield, with his 12 goals a decent return considering his horrendous barren run at the beginning of the campaign.

And now he was focused solely on success in the FA Cup final, and the chance to finally get his hands on a medal he believed he would have fully earned.

The only senior honour he had previously won was a First Division champions' medal during his stint at Norwich. But, as he spent only three months on loan at Carrow Road during that season, he felt that was a gong awarded to him almost by default. So he was determined to end his first season at Anfield with something tangible to show for his efforts.

He admitted in an interview with the *News of the World*, 'I won a championship medal with Norwich when I was on loan there from Aston Villa. But I only played a handful of games for them so I felt a bit of a fraud. I took the medal anyway, but if we can beat West Ham in the FA Cup final this one will be for real.

'One of the reasons I came to Liverpool was to be part of a club who win things and who challenge for honours.

This is hopefully the start for me and I want to look back with fond memories and winners' medals. This is going to be my first FA Cup final and I want to go away a winner.'

But Crouch refused to be swayed by the hype that suggested that all Liverpool needed to do was turn up on the day in Cardiff to claim their seventh FA Cup success.

He continued, 'People are saying that we are European champions and third in the league with a big squad and the money, so that should mean we will beat West Ham. But that is not the case.

'Credit to West Ham, they have been superb this season. A lot of people think that teams coming up from the Championship will automatically be involved in the relegation battle but that has never been the case for West Ham. And that's a credit to Alan Pardew and a credit to their players.'

The fact that Crouch was approaching the final as an integral part of the team was testimony to the strength of character he had showed during the dark days at the start of the season, and also vindication of the faith Benitez had shown in him during those troubled times.

And Crouch was quick to pay tribute to his boss. He said, 'The manager is top class. When I wasn't scoring goals I tried not to make a big issue of it. That's when Rafa came into his own. I had to make sure I was playing well and doing something for the team and, thankfully, the goals finally came.

'I was an easy target. There was a time I was really angry and I was desperate to prove wrong those people who had been critical of me. I even felt there was some sort of agenda to have a go at me; I realise now it was not the case, but it was pretty annoying at the time. I definitely have a smile on my face now because I believe I have proved people wrong.

'I suppose I have discovered an inner strength that has got me through the bad times. I was determined to succeed at this club. Not scoring was frustrating, but it has been a good season and it could end on a real high.'

And end on a high it did – in the most remarkable fashion. Not that it looked as though it would in the early stages in Cardiff.

A Carragher own goal and Dean Ashton's close-range poke, following an uncharacteristic error by Reina, handed West Ham a 2–0 lead after just 28 minutes and it looked as though Liverpool would end the season without a trophy to show for their efforts.

Cisse dragged them back into the contest with a goal after 32 minutes and, when Gerrard levelled the scores nine minutes after the break, it looked as though the favourites would prevail.

But Reina than allowed Paul Konchesky's speculative cross-cum-shot to loop over his head and into the net and Liverpool were once again on the back foot.

And there they stayed until the very last seconds of normal time when Gerrard unleashed a stunning volley from 30 yards that flew past Shaka Hislop in the West Ham goal to break the hearts of the Londoners and force the match into extra-time.

There were no further goals during the additional 30 minutes, ensuring that the drama would continue right until the last moment with a dramatic penalty shoot-out. And having won the Champions League final in exactly the same circumstances just 12 months earlier – on that occasion having dragged themselves back from an even more unlikely position – Liverpool were surely favourites once more.

And so it proved, as the pressure finally told on West Ham. Bobby Zamora, Konchesky and Anton Ferdinand all saw their penalties saved by Reina as he made amends for his earlier blunders as Liverpool triumphed 3–1 in the penalty shoot-out in a contest many have claimed to have been the best FA Cup final of modern times.

Afterwards, Benitez paid tribute to his weary troops. He said, 'I must give credit to my players as, after a 62-game season, a lot of them had cramp, but they kept going until the end, never gave up and have done a fantastic job.

'Steven Gerrard scored two fantastic goals and you know the quality he has and I give him credit, but for me it was the success of the team. Steven would say that himself and the energy levels the players showed was amazing. It was a fantastic final.'

For Crouch himself, the final did not perhaps go quite as he would have liked. As always he worked tirelessly for the team, but he couldn't find a goal to show for his efforts, and was withdrawn for Didi Hamman after 71 minutes as Benitez looked to shore up his side's midfield.

But, although the day belonged to Gerrard, Crouch had ended the season with what he wanted – a medal he could truly call his own and one he had worked so hard for. Indeed, had it not been for his dramatic winner against Manchester United in the fifth round, the story could have been all so different.

And so it was that he completed his first season at

Anfield with the first major honour of his career, having proved the doubters wrong and established himself as a key figure in the Liverpool squad.

But there was to be no resting on his laurels, nor any basking in the glory of his achievements. Instead, he had another important date to prepare for – the World Cup finals.

CHAPTER 6

GERMANY AND THE THREE LIONS

In October 2005, you would have been offered long odds at the bookmakers on Peter Crouch's chances of travelling to Germany for the World Cup finals as part of England's first-choice attack. It says much about the man that this is exactly what happened.

Having made his international debut against Colombia on the post-season tour of the USA in May 2005, shortly after his battling, but futile, attempts to save Southampton from relegation from the Premiership, Crouch had not been involved in the first three internationals of the 2005–06 season.

Perhaps that was a blessing in disguise for the man who was at that time trying to find his feet at Liverpool, because to say that England had performed below expectation would be something of an understatement.

They began the season – a season they hoped would end in World Cup glory on 9 July in Berlin – with an embarrassing 4–1 defeat in Denmark, England's heaviest loss for 25 years. Substitute goalkeeper David James shouldered most of the blame after conceding all four goals, having replaced Paul Robinson at half-time.

The keeper admitted that he had not prepared properly for the match, but the performance suggested that his teammates hadn't either. It did not augur well for a potential World Cup-winning campaign just ten months away.

Of course, England still had to qualify for the finals, but with four qualifiers remaining – away trips to Wales and Northern Ireland and home games against Austria and Poland – there didn't seem to be too much to be concerned about.

However, the alarm bells, while maybe not ringing loudly, would have been chiming quietly after a less-than-convincing display at the Millennium Stadium which saw them edge past Wales 1–0, courtesy of Joe Cole's second-half strike. It was not, though, the commanding performance of potential World Cup winners.

But, with the three points safely tucked away, Eriksson's men moved on to Belfast and a clash with Northern Ireland and what everyone expected would be a routine victory en route to Germany. The Irish, however, hadn't read the script.

In fairness, Eriksson's side were awful, but take nothing away from the Irish who beat England on home soil for the first time in 78 years, courtesy of David Healy's solitary strike. In years to come, expect there to be around 100,000 Irishmen claiming to have been at Windsor Park on that famous September night.

To compound England's misery, Wayne Rooney picked

up a booking during the defeat that would rule him out of the next qualifier at home to Austria a month later. The Manchester United man's absence, however, meant a chance for Crouch.

And there were many within the game who felt it was a chance he was well capable of taking. Former Southampton great Matt Le Tissier, a man who had watched Crouch at close quarters at St Mary's, told the media, 'Being without Wayne Rooney leaves a massive hole up front. We need someone to partner Michael Owen and I'd certainly go for Crouch – I think he's a good choice and he'll do really well.

'I know Peter's not scored yet this season – I'm sure he'll soon hit the target. But, even so, he does have a big input in games. His style causes problems for any defence and I can see him being a real handful for the Austrians, both in the air and on the deck.'

Former Portsmouth boss Graham Rix, the man who paid over a million pounds to take Crouch from QPR to Fratton Park, also backed him to succeed. And he even believed he could keep Rooney out of the starting line-up once he was free from suspension.

Rix told national newspaper journalists, 'Because he is so tall it is easy to write him off as just another target man, but ironically he is much better on the ground than he is in the air. He gives England something different, something that Michael Owen and even Wayne Rooney do not offer.

'He will cause any defence in the world problems and will be the perfect partner for Owen. The thought of Peter getting on the end of David Beckham's crosses is a mouthwatering one. It will be interesting to see what Sven does when Wayne is available again. If Peter plays as well as he can do, there is no reason he should not keep his place.'

So, even though he had failed to find the target for Liverpool, the striker was handed a starting berth against the Austrians – his first international on home soil – as Michael Owen's strike partner.

As he approached his competitive debut for his country, he told the *Evening Standard*, 'It would mean a lot to score for England. I have played one game in the States and really enjoyed that. Obviously to score would be a great feeling, with my family in the crowd and in such an important game. I would be as excited as anyone.

'As a forward, you have to be scoring goals but we [Liverpool] have been playing one up front sometimes and you have to do a lot of work for the team – and I have been doing that. There is no doubt in my mind that the goals will come, so I am not too concerned.

'It will be nice to play up front with someone like Michael Owen and, with David Beckham's crossing ability and creative play, it would be great to get on the end of a few crosses.'

Crouch rewarded Eriksson's faith with a performance of great promise, as he linked up well with Owen, continuing the chemistry the pair had demonstrated against the Colombians in America, a match in which Owen had scored a hat-trick.

Crouch created the first meaningful opening of the match when his perfect through-ball sent Owen clear and he was denied only by a last-ditch tackle from Paul Scharner. Midway through the first half, Crouch again provided

Owen with an opening, this time heading down for the Newcastle striker, and this time England were rewarded.

Although Owen himself was unable to finish the chance, that was only because he was hauled to the ground by Scharner. Referee Luis Medina Cantalejo of Spain had no hesitation in awarding a penalty, and Frank Lampard gratefully accepted the opportunity to settle England's nerves from the penalty spot.

But the home side were not having things all their own way and Austria had one or two chances of their own. And when David Beckham was sent off just before the hour mark, having committed two fouls inside a minute on Andreas Ibertsberger, the Three Lions were forced to play the remaining half hour with just ten men.

They defended resolutely, though, to claim all three points and ensure that, despite the setback of that defeat in Belfast, qualification remained in their hands. Victory over Poland in the second of the qualification double header on the following Wednesday night would book England's place in Germany.

For Crouch, his first game in an England shirt in England had ended in victory. And, although he did not score, he did enough to suggest he could be a genuine threat at the highest level.

Eriksson was certainly pleased with his efforts. The Swede said in his after-match press conference, 'As a performance I think we played very well and I'm very happy with the boys. I think Peter was effective. He is a young boy and has not played many times. But he was fighting, running and jumping – and many of the chances we created were from the long balls to him.'

Crouch, too, was encouraged by his debut in a competitive international, and particularly by his link-up with Owen. He told the media ranks at Old Trafford, 'We have to go into the Poland game with the same attitude. We have to be confident after this win and hopefully we will get a few more goals.

'It was good with Michael. It works well, he's a top-class player and I enjoy playing with him. It was disappointing, really, that it [the partnership] got broken up, because after the sending-off we had to change to a different formation.

'At the end it was difficult up there on my own. But I thought we coped with it well – and we got the result and that's what matters.'

In fact, later that evening that result took on even greater significance and ensured that England could approach the game against Poland in a relaxed frame of mind. Holland's victory over the Czech Republic later that Saturday night – the result apparently came through just as the England squad was sitting down to dinner in Manchester – meant that Eriksson's men were guaranteed a place in Germany as one of the two best runners-up from the European qualifying groups, regardless of the result against Poland.

All that remained now was to end the campaign in style with a win over the Poles to confirm their place at the top of the group.

Eriksson said, 'I'm delighted that we now know we will be taking part in the World Cup in Germany next year. It has been a difficult start to the season for us but, together with our victory against Austria, this is the reward for all the hard work that has been done over the past year. Our win today showed the character and determination we have in this group of players. They were focused.

'The fans have played a huge part in every game. No other team enjoys such incredible support and our qualification is due also to them. I know that the whole nation will get behind the team at the World Cup. I hope we can deliver the kind of success the fans deserve.

'We still have a very important match on Wednesday against Poland and we will now be focusing all our efforts on winning that match and finishing top of the group.'

But, while England basked in the glory of a qualifying job well done, there still remained dissenting voices – among the fans and the media – that were unhappy with the balance of Eriksson's side and their unconvincing recent displays.

And Crouch was coming in for more than his fair share of criticism, with the doubters claiming that a man who couldn't score for his club should not be playing for his country and insisting that he lacked the pace to succeed at international level.

Indeed, one internet joke doing the rounds went like this: 'Sven is facing the firing squad. He is asked if he has any last requests. 'One,' he says. 'I'd like Peter Crouch to take the shot!'

Whatever the critics may have been saying, however, Eriksson's opinion was the only one that counted. And he clearly believed Crouch deserved his place in the international fold.

However, the striker had to be content with a place on the bench when England lined up against Poland, making way for the returning Rooney to partner Owen in attack.

It was Owen who gave England the lead two minutes before half-time, only for substitute Tomasz Frankowski to cancel out that advantage on the stroke of half-time. But England got the win they wanted when Lampard volleyed home Owen's cross ten minutes from time to end the qualification process on a high.

But while the team took the plaudits for securing their safe passage to Germany, much of the post-match coverage focused on the treatment dished out by the fans to Crouch when he replaced Shaun Wright-Phillips with a little over 20 minutes of the Polish match to go.

His introduction was met with a chorus of boos and whistles as the fans let Eriksson know what they thought of his decision to send on the Liverpool striker. Afterwards, however, the head coach remained unrepentant and resolute in his defence of Crouch.

He insisted in his post-match press conference, 'I understand the crowd in the sense that Shaun Wright-Phillips gave us flair and beat people, but I think it was the right decision as he got a bad knock and he wasn't 100 per cent right.

'When you need to score with 25 minutes to go, why not try Crouch and play with three strikers? It worked well this time, who knows next time?

'I don't know who was being booed, whether it was me or Peter Crouch, but we won the game and I'm sorry if anyone thinks Peter Crouch is a not a good footballer.'

Crouch's team-mates were also quick to stick up for the striker. Joe Cole told the press, 'It was ridiculous. Peter is a great player. He is an important member of the squad and is going to have some great moments in an England shirt. The booing of Peter on Wednesday night was not good. Unfortunately, people believe what they read in the papers.'

Match winner Lampard added, 'What happened was unfortunate. Crouchy did very well for us the other day against Austria. He was very effective and I think he has been very effective for Liverpool. We have to get behind people, especially young players coming in and playing their first few games.

'I hope what happened doesn't affect Crouchy's confidence. He is a good player and he'll be a good player for England.'

The pressure was still on Crouch a month later, however, as England travelled to Geneva to take on Argentina in a showpiece friendly as their preparations for the World Cup finals began in earnest.

Eriksson, though, did his best to convince the doubters that Crouch was worthy of his place in the squad ahead of the game. He insisted, 'It's a pity when he gets booed. I would say to the fans that he will not get better by being booed. He's a very good boy, very honest and very hard working.

'He covered more ground than any other player against Austria, which is strange for a centre-forward. Of course I would like to see him score goals, but he is still a danger man who creates problems. He is not the most elegant of players, but he is very special – more special than any other player I've had.'

In a fantastic match, a welcome contrast to the vast majority of friendlies during Eriksson's reign, England ran out 3–2 winners. Hernan Crespo gave the Argentines the lead in the 35th minute, only for Rooney to level the scores just three minutes later.

Defender Walter Samuel made it 2–1 to the South Americans nine minutes after half-time, but England snatched victory in an astonishing finale as Owen stole in to score twice in the last three minutes.

By that time, Crouch had replaced full-back Luke Young as England searched for a way back into the game and it was the big striker's presence in the box that seemed to induce total panic in the Argentinean backline, who up until that point had looked relatively untroubled.

But they were clearly terrified of Crouch's aerial threat, and he created the space for Owen to capitalise and seal a memorable victory simply by being in the box.

And it was a buoyant David Beckham who told thefa.com that this would be the benchmark by which England's players would judge themselves at the finals. 'If we perform like that in the World Cup finals, then we'll be happy,' he said. 'This was a special occasion, these games against Argentina always are. We can't get too carried away with the result, but we'll enjoy the performance and we'll enjoy the result for now.

'I said at half-time that it felt like a World Cup qualifier or a World Cup game. That was the atmosphere that was made by the fans, the opposition and the spirit that we played in. All the way through the game we created chances. It wasn't just the three goals that we scored, but there were lots of others, too.

'That was the pleasing thing. But the most important and pleasing thing was the passion and pride the whole team showed. The togetherness we showed in first of all coming back from 1–0 and then 2–1 down made it a great overall performance.'

It meant England ended the calendar year with an overall record of having played 11 games, won eight of them, drawn one and lost two. Not bad, but there was certainly room for improvement and there would need to be if they were to mount a genuine challenge for the top honour in Germany.

With that in mind, England's first appearance of 2006 – and their last game before Eriksson had to name his World Cup squad – pitted them against Uruguay, one of the top South American nations, though surprisingly they would be absent from that summer's finals.

Still, they were expected to provide a stern test for Eriksson's side and that was how it transpired. With Owen having broken a bone in his foot against Tottenham on New Year's Eve, Darren Bent was given his chance up front alongside Rooney. But, when England needed a saviour, it was Crouch who came up with the goods to silence the boo-boys.

On this occasion, it must be said, he received unequivocal support from the home crowd with the game being staged at Anfield. But his impact, having replaced Rooney as a 63rd-minute substitute, reverberated far wider than merely within the immediate surroundings on Merseyside. This was the night that Crouch truly arrived as an international footballer.

At the time of his introduction, England were trailing to Omar Pousa's stunning 30-yard volley, but within 12 minutes of taking the field the Liverpool striker had restored parity.

His confidence had been boosted just ten days earlier with his FA Cup winner against Manchester United, and it would have been sky high when he headed home his first England goal from Joe Cole's cross to equalise.

And Crouch's, and England's, night was complete, when Cole himself fired home the winner three minutes into injury time as he converted a cross from Wright-Phillips, another sub who had entered the fray at the same time as Crouch.

It provided the perfect confidence booster for the squad with the World Cup just four months away, and for Crouch, in particular, it was an especially sweet evening.

He told journalists after the match, 'The fans were great with me in the Argentina game and I think they were always going to be good to me at Anfield. Hopefully, the goal will prove a lot of the doubters wrong.

'The manager never doubted me. Maybe other people did, but he has always had confidence in me. He put me in squads and I have a lot to thank him for. I feel like an international player in the company of my team-mates. If I didn't, I wouldn't be here.

'I want to perform well for Liverpool and look forward to the World Cup, like everyone else in that dressing room. You want to start, but I am realistic and Wayne Rooney and Michael Owen are top-class players who will start ahead of me. If I can play some role, then I will be happy.

'It worked against Uruguay when I came off the bench to score and we've won the game. It's harder to come off the bench, but if there's some role to be played then I will do it because I want to be part of the England set-up.'

Once again, his team-mates were quick to sing his

praises. Captain Beckham said, 'He does well for us when he plays and he has deserved his chance. It is tough when you first come into a team. You have to win people over and he has done it with the players, without a doubt.'

Eriksson, too, was in bullish mood after seeing Crouch vindicate his decision to stick by him, despite fierce criticism from other quarters. He insisted, 'Peter Crouch showed, once again, that he is important even when he sits on the bench. He was involved a lot against Argentina and scored tonight.

'That's Peter Crouch, he's different. Even when he came on I don't think we used him as well as we should have done. We had chances to cross and free-kicks out wide where we kept possession instead of putting it in directly. He is almost impossible to defend against when the delivery is right.'

It was becoming increasingly clear that, whatever the sceptics might say, Crouch would be going to the World Cup finals as one of the best 23 footballers in the country. Eriksson had obviously decided that, even if his role was merely to be that of an impact player coming off the bench, Crouch was a player he wanted with him in Germany.

And, with Owen seemingly on the road to recovery in plenty of time for the finals, Eriksson's attacking options looked good, with the likes of Crouch, Bent and Jermain Defoe as back-up to the first-choice pairing of Owen and Rooney, a world-class duo any country would be delighted to have.

But the Swede's plans were dealt a hammer blow on 30 April when Rooney broke his metatarsal in a clash with

Chelsea's Paulo Ferreira. All of a sudden, England's plans were in tatters.

Rooney's injury devastated the nation and meant that, when Eriksson named his 23-man party for the finals, he would be taking a huge gamble on the fitness of two of his key attackers – Owen and Rooney.

By the time England lined up for their penultimate friendly before the squad departed for Germany, against Hungary, Owen was fit enough to take his place in the team. But having played just 30 minutes of Newcastle's last game of the season – a month previously – and an hour in England's 'B' friendly against Belarus the week before the Hungary match, it was plain to see that, after four months out, Owen was far from match fit.

So it was perhaps even stranger that he was handed a lone striking role, with Joe Cole playing in the 'hole' behind him. And the sight of Jamie Carragher in an unfamiliar midfield role would have Eriksson's critics, of which there were many, sharpening their pencils in readiness to write his World Cup obituary.

In the end, though, it turned out to be a decent night for England. They won comfortably enough and there were two memorable firsts – a first goal for his country for John Terry and a first senior appearance for Arsenal youngster Theo Walcott, who became England's youngest ever player, having been astonishingly called into the World Cup squad at the eleventh hour; this despite the fact that he was just 17 years old and yet to play in the Premiership.

Eriksson had described the former Southampton youngster's call-up at the time as 'a gamble', and it was one that would backfire spectacularly on the Swede. But that was for the future.

In the present, England beat Hungary 3–1 and Crouch again came off the bench to make an impact – scoring the third goal six minutes from time with an excellent finish after some superb approach play.

But if his goal was special, a sweetly struck right-footed shot from 18 yards, his celebration was even more memorable as he launched into an extraordinary robotic dance that he had first demonstrated at David and Victoria Beckham's pre-World Cup bash the week before.

Crouch confessed, 'Unsurprisingly, there had been a bit of banter about it and I just wanted to do it again.'

And Eriksson was happy with what he had seen from his side, and from Crouch – his performance anyway, not necessarily his dancing! He told the media, 'We were even better than I thought we would be. Hungary are a technically good side. They keep the ball well, break forward and they scored a fantastic goal, I must say.

'It was a very good test for us and I'm rather happy with it, although I'm sure we'll be playing even better at the World Cup. It's important that we were patient, because we were up against a team with nine men behind the ball, so we couldn't win the ball and play it forward very quickly. It's very difficult because you don't find any spaces anywhere.

'We started the second half very well and scored two good goals from set-pieces to make it 2–0. Set-pieces are important to us, because we have people other than David Beckham who can take them, and then in the box we are physically strong and have very good headers of the ball and players who can score goals.

'Peter scored a great goal. More or less every time he plays for England he does a good job. Peter is a very special footballer. He is extremely useful. What I particularly like is how hard he works for the team during a game. He is good with the ball on the floor and will scare defenders in the air.'

England's preparations were set to continue with their final warm-up match against Jamaica at Old Trafford four days after the Hungary game, but before that they had a very special visitor to their Manchester training camp – Prince William.

And while the future king of England was keen to see the lads being put through their paces and to get the lowdown on Eriksson's tactics for Germany, the one thing he really wanted to see was ... Peter Crouch dance!

And so it was that the big forward found himself performing his new celebration routine – already dubbed 'the Crouch' – in front of the heir to the throne.

And afterwards he had to admit that he had felt a little embarrassed. He told the media, 'He's the future king of England and I've just done a dance in front of him. It's a bit surreal. I don't know how the guys talked me into it to be honest. They were goading me on quite a bit. He seemed quite happy. He spoke to us afterwards and he's looking forward to the World Cup as much as the rest of us.'

Crouch's relaxed attitude, however, and his willingness to clown around in front of Prince William, was further proof that he finally felt part of the England set-up and that he had overcome the stick he received in the early days of his international career.

He added, 'There's a lot of pressure on us going into the World Cup and we're just trying to relax in any way we can before such a big tournament. It's just a bit of fun we've had between the lads that seems to have escalated a touch. It shows there's a good team spirit.

'I feel really at home in the England set-up and it shows on the pitch. If you feel comfortable in your surroundings, you'll perform better on the pitch and that's definitely the case with myself.'

And Crouch promised that his robot dance would be back if he found the target against Jamaica. 'If everyone's pleased with it and everyone finds it funny then I'm sure I'll keep on doing it,' he admitted. 'There's enough pressure on the lads without celebrations being pressurised as well.'

There was not too much pressure around at Old Trafford during the Jamaica match as England ran out confident 6–0 winners. But there was plenty of evidence of the robot dance as Crouch helped himself to a hat-trick.

And with further goals from Lampard, Owen and a Jermaine Taylor own goal, England completed their warm-up for Germany in fine style.

In fact, the afternoon could have been even better for Crouch as he could have had a fourth goal. At that stage of the game he had scored only twice, but he wasted the chance of a treble by trying an extravagant chip from the penalty spot that sailed spectacularly over the bar.

Fortunately for him, he had the chance to complete his hat-trick a minute from time – a chance he gratefully accepted – but that was not enough to save him from a dressing down from Eriksson.

The Swede said in his post-match media briefing, 'I must criticise Peter's penalty. It was a golden chance to practise spot-kicks before Germany and he joked about it. He apologised afterwards and if it had been a penalty shoot-out I doubt if he'd try to do the same. Yes, you can miss a penalty – but not the way he did.'

Crouch's treble clearly put him in pole position for the opening World Cup game against Paraguay a week later and Eriksson admitted as much when he said, 'Peter did a fantastic job. He did almost everything – linking the play, holding the ball up and scoring.

'Peter has always been in my thoughts. It's difficult to mark him. When the ball is high in the air, sometimes a defender can't do anything but foul him.'

Crouch himself kept tight-lipped about his penalty blunder, but he was enthused by the team's overall display. He said, 'It's a great send-off for the lads and it bodes well for Germany. It is a terrific feeling to get a hat-trick for England. We looked like a proper team and that's a big plus before the World Cup.'

And captain Beckham insisted Crouch's hat-trick marked his full arrival as an international star. He added, 'We're all pleased for Peter. He was booed by fans in our match against Austria last autumn, which was uncalled for. But it was totally different here. He's not just a great lad and a great player but he's also a great scorer – and he showed that.'

As for his robotic celebrations, they were the subject of a less serious World Cup campaign – novelty bets.

William Hill's spokesman Graham Sharpe said, 'It is our top novelty bet. It has eclipsed interest in what haircut Beckham will be sporting for the opening game. We are offering odds of 2/1 that he will perform it once in the tournament, 3/1 to bring it out twice and 4/1 for three or more. We have already seen bets of £500.'

William Hill even offered odds of 50/1 that Crouch would win television dance contest *Strictly Come Dancing*!

Crouch was also immortalised as a *Subbuteo* figure, as MB Games rushed out a mini-Crouch. Not because of his goalscoring prowess, though, but because of his celebration!

A spokesman for the games company said, 'The "Crouchbop" has made its way into the public consciousness, so it seems like the right thing to do. The World Cup is only five days away, but we are working flat out to get the figure out.'

For the England squad, however, it was time for the fun and games to stop as they made final preparations for their journey to their World Cup base in Baden-Baden, a base they hoped to remain at all the way through to the World Cup final itself in Berlin on 9 July.

And for Eriksson, as he approached his last few weeks in the England job before handing over the reins to his assistant Steve McClaren, there was genuine belief that the campaign would end in glory.

He insisted, 'I think the chances of winning the World Cup are very, very good. I have always said that and I still believe that.'

And, even with the continuing fitness doubts over Rooney, England's players were in confident mood, particularly after having seen Crouch net four goals in his last two internationals.

Rio Ferdinand said, 'It was great to see him score a hat-trick against Jamaica, even though he missed a penalty. He and Michael played really well together. Crouchy's a great lad. I've known him through the years and he's always had a smile on his face. He plays like that as well.'

Joe Cole also confirmed he was a member of the Peter Crouch fan club, telling the media, 'It was fantastic to see Peter score a hat-trick. He is a great player and I think people are finally seeing his character coming through.

'He is playing with a smile on his face and we always believed in him and knew what a great talent he was. Now everyone else is seeing it. I think Peter has always done well for England. He has had a great start to his international career. He played in America and set up goals for Michael Owen and came on against Argentina and made a big difference.

'He has now scored a hat-trick and I don't know why people get the impression he has not done anything. He has had a fantastic start [to his international career] and has always done well. You can come in from the left and clip the ball up to him and there is always a chance he is going to knock the ball down. He gives the team different options.

'He signed for Liverpool and had a great season there. He won the FA Cup and has now had a magical start to his England career. He is a top-drawer player.'

And Cole's Chelsea team-mate Frank Lampard reckoned that, even without Rooney, England had the firepower to succeed thanks to Crouch and Owen.

He told the press, 'Crouch and Owen play off each other really well. Peter is a very intelligent player and a great target man. Michael likes to get in behind the defence and it was nice to see them link up well together against Jamaica.

'I think Peter deserves all the credit he is getting at the moment. People are not just seeing that Crouchy is a very good player but seeing the character from within.

'He is a great lad and always has a smile on his face, which is a good thing because it helps everyone watching him play. He is great for team spirit and you need characters like that.

'You have to forget about his size and stature and remember he has got a great touch, great feet and a clever brain. I think him and Michael suit each other really well.'

And there were plenty of people from outside the England camp keen to stress that Crouch had the ability to make an impact at the World Cup.

His former boss Harry Redknapp told the national media, 'I can see Peter being in the starting line-up, certainly for England's group games, and he will cope, no doubt about it. Whether it is as a lone striker with five across midfield, or with a partner like Michael Owen, he will be up to the task.

'I would love to see him given the opportunity because his game is about far more than being a target man. His touch is great and he has the ability to hold the ball up and bring other people into the game. And not too many defenders at the finals will ever have come up against a player like Crouchy. They will find him a real handful.

'Even when he was going through that barren spell [at

Liverpool] and received a bit of stick, he was not the sort to hide. He stood up to be counted. That shows the character of the guy and shows why I know he will not be fazed by the World Cup finals.'

Liverpool manager Rafael Benitez agreed, adding, 'What you must remember is how he dealt with things when he went all those games without scoring a goal. People were talking and talking, but he continued working hard and playing well and he has scored 12 goals this season.

'He has enough quality and experience for England. He has the temperament and he can handle the responsibility. He has confidence in himself.'

Jack Charlton, a member of the 1966 World Cup-winning side, was also backing the Liverpool front man to come good in Germany and compensate for the loss of Rooney.

He told the *Newcastle Evening Chronicle*, 'Yes, England have a smashing chance if Wayne Rooney is fit, and even if he isn't they will still have a shout because they can play Peter Crouch alongside Michael Owen and change everything tactically, creating a new set of problems for the opposition.

'Rooney is terrific for a lad of 20. He's quick and strong, a great striker of the ball and not a bad header either. As a defender you can't leave him alone for a moment. He drops off, links up play, goes wide and sprints through the middle. A total handful.

'I wanted to bet on England winning the European Championship two years ago until Rooney got himself injured. I blame the modern boots for all the metatarsal injuries that have hit Rooney, Owen and the like. We never got them in my day because the tongue on a boot was so long we could fold it back over as extra protection.

'But if Rooney doesn't make it then England must not leave Owen on his own. He's quick and looks to utilise space in the box, but without Rooney he would need that extra help. Crouch is perfect under those circumstances.

'Central defenders are no longer 6ft 3in giants and they're bothered by genuine height. Two men would have to be employed against Crouch, which is excellent for the darting Owen. That's how he scored at the near post against Argentina a little while back. Crouch had taken two defenders to the far post with him.

'Crouch can change the angle of England's attack, just as Niall Quinn did for me with the Republic of Ireland. Niall wanted to be a player and join in, but I wanted to get him to the back post because the opposition dare not leave him one-on-one with a little full-back. Kevin Phillips has never scored as many goals as he did at Sunderland with Quinn, and Owen can do the same with Crouch.'

And while those around him, and those outside the camp, had confidence in Crouch, he and his team-mates, as well as the England management team, certainly had the collective confidence that they could go all the way in Germany.

On the eve of the opening Group B game against Paraguay, Eriksson spoke in glowing terms of his players and of their chance to make history and become the first English side to win the trophy on foreign soil.

He insisted, 'Everything looks very good, I must say. The players are in good shape physically and in good form. They are very, very confident. Of course, it's important to take three points, which I strongly believe we will. It will send out a message to other countries and be good for the confidence in this World Cup. Once again, I believe that we can win it.'

And the England head coach also had words of encouragement for Crouch and confirmed that he would start alongside Owen in the absence of the recovering Rooney, just eight months after he had been booed on to the Old Trafford pitch against Poland.

Eriksson added, 'Peter Crouch will be completely different to Rooney, you can't compare them because the style is completely different. But he is ready for this stage. He and Michael are a very good couple. I am sure they will create problems for any team in the world today.'

But for all the bullish talk ahead of the game, England were less than convincing against the South Americans. True, they got the win they wanted, and at this stage of the tournament that is what counted, with pundits and commentators queuing up to insist there was no point peaking too soon, but the reality was the performance lacked cohesion and inspiration.

Having been gifted a dream start when Carlos Gamarra headed Beckham's free-kick into his own net, England failed to capitalise. They dominated possession in the first half without creating too many clear-cut chances, but they faded badly after the interval and were left hanging on to their slender advantage at the end.

For Crouch it had been a frustrating afternoon. He battled hard to make things happen in attack, but was regularly penalised by Mexican referee Marco Rodriguez for aerial fouls that were, at best, innocuous, and which often looked as though it was the England man who was being sinned against.

The frustration finally got the better of him and he was booked for dissent after protesting once more about the referee's decision to penalise him.

He said after the game, 'When you jump you have to use your arms to get leverage, but it doesn't seem to be allowed. It's international football and you have to adapt. It was overly fussy at times, but I don't want to blame referees.

'I don't think there would have been one foul in the Premiership, but there were probably six or seven [given against me] in the first half, which was frustrating. The way I was brought up to play, it's not a foul. I am aware of it now and I don't think I will get pulled up as much in the next game.'

As for the team's overall display, there was widespread satisfaction that they had got the tournament off to a winning start and, while acknowledging that they faded after the half-time interval, they were quick to point out that there was one decisive factor – the heat.

Beckham insisted to journalists afterwards, 'People don't realise how hot it was out there. It was a three o'clock kick-off and is right in the middle the day. It was 28 or 29 degrees out there. But we'll be all right.

'We must perform better and play better, but we got what we wanted. We were good at times, but we gave away the ball too much. The performance could be better but we will work on that. We set out to get the three points and we did that. But we were exhausted. We can put it down to that [the heat] because we are usually strong and our fitness levels are high.'

The good news for England was that their two remaining group games, against Trinidad & Tobago and Sweden, would be played in the evening, thus nullifying the effects of the unseasonably hot temperatures in Germany.

But there could be no doubt that there was much to work on before the Trinidad game, a match in which a number of English lower-league players would be seeking to make a name for themselves against their more illustrious adversaries.

And if England needed a warning that they would not have things all their own way against the tiny Caribbean nation – the smallest country ever to qualify for a World Cup finals – it came in Trinidad's first match against Sweden when they earned a superb battling 0–0 draw, despite having to play for virtually the whole of the second half with only ten men after Avery John was sent off in the 46th minute.

But the disappointing nature of the Paraguay game had done nothing to erode the confidence in the England camp, and they approached the Trinidad encounter still firmly believing they were on the right path to success.

Crouch told a pre-match media gathering, 'We all believe going into the next couple of games we will get the right results. The important game is the next one because if we win it we go through. It's always going to be difficult in a World Cup against anyone, and Trinidad proved that in the Sweden game. But we want to finish top of our group.

You didn't see us at our best on Saturday with the way the game went and I'm sure that you'll see a different team during the later kick-offs and not a tired team. We can take heart from our first-half performance when Paraguay never threatened at all. We felt we were much the better side and that we could go on and score three or four.

'At half-time we were cooling down the best we could, but when we got out for the second half the heat did affect us a bit too much. Now the kick-offs are later you'll hopefully see better from us throughout the 90 minutes, rather than just the first half.'

Victory over Trinidad & Tobago would mean England equalling their post-war record of eight successive wins and the team was given a massive boost on the eve of the game when Eriksson announced that Rooney was ready to play a part.

The Manchester United star had been expected to be ruled out until at least the quarter-finals, but he had recovered much quicker from his broken metatarsal than was initially expected and was named among the substitutes. Eriksson insisted, 'For me, Rooney is match fit.'

The Swede also denied that he had been involved in a furious bust-up with FA chief executive Brian Barwick over the use of Rooney in the tournament. He added, 'It's been reported that Brian and I had a row about it, that's completely a lie. We have discussed it a lot in a positive way, but have had absolutely no disputes at all.'

The vast majority of England fans back home and in Germany, though, while delighted to hear the news that Rooney was fit again, hoped that he would not be needed against Trinidad. After all, if England could not beat a team ranked outside the world's top 100 without him, what chance did they have in the rest of the tournament?

Eriksson certainly expected an improved team display and nothing less than a win. He told the press, 'We are going to play the best football we can from the first minute. The first game we were a little knocked out in the second half by the heat but now we have practised in the heat so I think it will be better.

'I think we did everything we could to learn from that [Paraguay match]. After the game we even talked to a specialist about how much the players sweated and spent time finding out who was drinking enough water. I don't think in terms of nutrition or drinking we can do anything more.

'In the team talk there will be a lot about the Trinidad players being hungry and working hard. They put in an excellent performance against Sweden. It's up to us to make sure we play well.

'We want to win the group because it will be better for us. We did not finish top in Japan, Sweden did, or in Portugal when France did, so we want to improve. The players want to put in a good performance and I am sure we will do much better than we did on Saturday.'

But, once again, for all the confident talk in the build-up to the match, England failed to deliver. They were at least matched by a spirited Trinidad side in the first half and it was no surprise when, just 13 minutes into the second half, Rooney and Aaron Lennon were introduced as replacements for Owen and Carragher to try to inject some life into the England performance.

But it was Trinidad who looked the most likely team to open the scoring when substitute Cornell Glen broke clear. Only a magnificent last-ditch tackle from Ashley

Cole prevented him from testing Paul Robinson, and quite possibly giving the underdogs a shock lead.

And so England entered the last ten minutes desperately searching for the goal that would win them the game and book their place in the last 16. Finally, seven minutes from the end, it arrived.

Beckham swung in a deep cross from the right and Crouch rose highest at the far post to power home his header. This time he wasn't penalised for a foul, perhaps slightly fortuitously, as television replays later showed he had pulled the dreadlocks of Trinidad defender Brent Sancho when he climbed into the air.

But England weren't going to worry about that, and nor was Crouch, as the big centre-forward took his goals tally for England to six, with five of them coming in his last four internationals. There was no robot dance to celebrate this time, but the crucial thing was that England had made the breakthrough they needed.

Gerrard grabbed a second goal for England with a blistering left-foot drive a minute into injury time to make the final score 2–0, but there was no doubt that the result flattered England.

But, just as had been the case against Paraguay, the three points counted far more than the performance and, with two wins out of two, England had safely booked their passage into the last 16 before their final, and most testing, group game against Sweden.

And Crouch was delighted with his goal that set the team on their way. Still, he was quick to praise the part played by the team captain in the creation of the crucial header that broke the stalemate.

He said to reporters, 'David [Beckham] is the best in the world at delivering crosses, we all know that and everyone else can see that. It was a good result for us. We kept going to the end; that was the most important thing. Bringing on Wayne Rooney and Aaron Lennon gave us a boost, because we needed fresh legs to run at them. Six points out of two games is perfect for us and now we are in the next round.

'It was a big moment for me. It's great to score in a World Cup. I'm really enjoying it; I'm loving playing for England. With the creative players we have in the side you are always going to get chances and thankfully at the minute they are going in for me.'

Crouch was relieved to have finally broken the deadlock having squandered two good openings earlier in the game – a header and a volley – but he insisted that he didn't let those misses affect his performance.

He added, 'I was disappointed to miss the earlier chances, but you can't let your head drop, because with the delivery in our team, especially from Beckham, you are always going to get another chance. You have to keep plugging away.

'Sweden found to their cost that Trinidad put up a good fight. But, thankfully, we managed to break them down in the end. We're through to the next round already. However, we can't think about who we will get. We just have to win the next game.

'The game against Sweden now is the most important thing. We would love to have nine points out of nine. We have ground out results so far. However, if you had said at the start of the tournament that we'd have three goals, none conceded and six points, then we would have taken

At home at Anfield. Scoring the winning goal against Manchester United in February 2006.

Victory! Celebrating scoring the winner against Chelsea in the Community Shield in 2006.

Above: Champions League action. Crouch volleys the ball to score his second goal against Galatasaray and, *below*, acknowledges the fans.

For Queen and country – his home England debut against Austria.

A joyous day for Liverpool. Both fans and the players are over the moon at winning the FA Cup in 2006.

Crouch jumps for joy at scoring his first goal against Greece at Old Trafford.

bove: Scoring for his country against Andorra in the qualifiers for the European
hampionship.

elow: The infamous robot dance.

Above: The match during which Crouchy scored a hat-trick for England, against Jamaica.

Below: Crouch stands proudly in the England line up, head and shoulders above his fellow players.

it. We do know we can play better – and I'm sure we will do – but at the minute we are just enjoying this result.'

Eriksson was also pleased to be through the next round and, far from agreeing with much of the criticism that greeted his team's performance, he applauded their display against Trinidad.

He said, 'We had a lot of chances in the first 80 minutes and we were unlucky not to take them. Trinidad & Tobago defended with eight, nine or ten men behind the ball and made things very difficult for us. They showed great discipline and great strength, but we showed great patience, too. We fully deserved the win. Both goals we scored were excellent.'

Captain Beckham, though, admitted that England had been below par, but he assured the fans that the side would improve. He told a media conference, 'It would be fair to say that you have not seen the best of us yet, but we have got ourselves in a good position to qualify [as group winners].

'We know we can play better and there is better to come and we have to show people that.'

They would certainly need to play better in their final group game against Sweden if they were to prevail against a country they had not beaten since 1968. There would be no better place to put that record straight than in Cologne.

The match took on added significance as, with England already through to the last 16 and Sweden almost certain to join them – having beaten Paraguay in their second game – the group winners would most likely avoid host nation Germany, who were expected to beat Ecuador, who themselves had already qualified for the second round, in the next stage.

Not that England were prepared to admit they were thinking that far ahead. Beckham added, 'I don't think it matters once you are in the last 16 who you play, because every team you come up against deserves to be there and we can expect a very tough game. That's when the big games come.'

But for all the speed and skill that Ecuador had demonstrated in their opening two games – wins against Poland and Costa Rica – there was no doubt that England would prefer to face the South Americans rather than a German side that was gaining an all-too-familiar momentum and that had already won over a sceptical home support who had written off their chances before the start of the tournament.

So it was against that backdrop that England approached the Sweden game, and there were some bold selection decisions for Eriksson to confront, not least with regard to the fitness and availability of Rooney.

But, while he contemplated unleashing Rooney against his fellow countrymen, the Swedish camp were actually more concerned by the potential threat posed by Crouch.

Captain Olof Mellberg, who played with Crouch at Aston Villa, admitted that he and his fellow defenders were worried about the Liverpool man. He said of Rooney's injury, 'I don't even know which foot it is,' before adding at a pre-match media briefing, 'Maybe Crouch could end up causing us more problems.

'I have to say I am a bit surprised at how far he has

come since we were team-mates. He was on the bench a lot of the time at Villa and didn't make many starts at all. He ended up going to a smaller club, in Southampton, to get games, and obviously from there has done really well to get a move to Liverpool and now into the England side.

'It has been a very strange career for him. He even had a spell on loan with a small club in Sweden, but he has improved incredibly well over the past couple of seasons.'

In the end, Eriksson opted to start with Rooney and Owen up front, leaving Crouch on the bench to protect him from a possible suspension ahead of the last-16 match after he had picked up a booking in the first game against Paraguay. Gerrard, also on a yellow card after that clash against the South Americans, was also rested.

But just when it appeared that England's fitness worries were over, there was another crushing blow for the squad in just the first minute of the game against Sweden when Owen fell awkwardly and could only crawl to the side of the pitch in obvious agony.

England physio Gary Lewin immediately signalled to the bench that the striker was unable to continue, and so Crouch was quickly introduced into the action.

That decision, though, puzzled many spectators, given the fact that the Liverpool star had been left out in the first instance in order to ensure he didn't miss a more important match through suspension. So the question was posed: why bring him on after only a couple of minutes when Theo Walcott was also on the bench?

It merely highlighted the folly of Eriksson's decision to go into the tournament with only four strikers, two of whom – Owen and Rooney – were not fully fit, and one of them – Walcott – having not even played a Premiership game for Arsenal. It was a selection gamble that had failed badly.

As for the Sweden game itself, it followed a typical pattern. Twice England were in front, only to be pegged back right at the end by a foe they seem unable to conquer.

The match came alive in the 34th minute when Joe Cole controlled a clearance on his chest and unleashed a magnificent, unstoppable, dipping 30-yard volley that gave the goalkeeper no chance and flew into the top corner. It was a quite breathtaking strike by the Chelsea midfielder.

It was hoped that goal would provide the impetus for England to go on and claim victory but, once more, their fallibility after half-time was evident just six minutes into the second half when Marcus Allback rose above Beckham to head home a corner at the near post to make the scores level.

That goal certainly unsettled England and the midfield – where Owen Hargreaves had been inspired in the holding role – lost some of its shape and its grip on the game. Eriksson attempted to counter that by sending on Gerrard in place of the visibly tiring Rooney, and it was the Liverpool midfield star who looked to have conjured up the winner for England.

He had been on the pitch for less than 20 minutes when he met Joe Cole's cross with a bullet header to give England the lead with just five minutes remaining, admittedly very much against the run of play. Surely they had now confirmed top spot in the group and finally ended their near 40-year hoodoo against the Swedes?

Well, yes and no. They did indeed win Group B, but

they could not win the match. Instead, a long throw into England's penalty area in the final minute of normal time caused hesitancy in the defence and, as John Terry, Sol Campbell and Paul Robinson all looked on, it was veteran goalpoacher Henrik Larsson who stole in to flick the ball into the net to make the final scoreline 2–2.

Ultimately, it was not too damaging as England saw out the final couple of minutes of added time to confirm their place at the head of the group and book themselves a second-round date against Ecuador. Not only did that mean they had avoided Germany, but they would also now have an extra day's rest all the way through to the final itself, should they make it that far.

But, with the strikers struggling for goals – only Crouch had found the target in the three games so far – and Owen now ruled out for the remainder of the tournament with ruptured knee ligaments, England could ill afford the defensive frailties that had been exposed against the Swedes.

Even Eriksson, who until that point had remained supremely confident about his chances of ending his England managerial reign in a glorious finale, was forced to admit in his media conference after that draw, 'We didn't defend very well against set-pieces and we will have to work on it until the next game. Sweden are very strong in the air, but we have to do much better in the future. Normally we are very good on that, we concede very little from set-pieces, but today – two goals.'

But, despite the doom and gloom caused by a less-than-convincing series of performances in the group stages, and the horrendous injury suffered by Owen, other teams at the tournament still believed England had a good chance of lifting the trophy.

After seeing for himself the threat posed by the Three Lions, Mellberg insisted, 'I think England can still go a long way in Germany. They look really strong to me and have a good variety in their game. They mix it up.

'Normally they are very strong on set-pieces and they have pace and strength up front, have good defenders and in Lampard and Gerrard they have outstanding midfielders coming into the box. They look strong all over.'

And the Swedish defender reckoned England could cope without Owen, and backed Crouch and Rooney to score the goals to fire England to glory. He added in his media conference, 'I think they can get over the loss of Michael Owen. I think Rooney and Crouchy can be a threat to any of the remaining teams.

'They complement each other so well, with Crouchy's strength in the air and Rooney's all-round strength. They can be very dangerous.'

Crouch himself was also keen to continue to make an impact in the tournament and was happy to shoulder the burden of responsibility for leading the line in the absence of Owen.

He told the press, 'I have enjoyed playing in the tournament. Scoring in the World Cup finals was a great achievement, but I do not want to rest on that. Hopefully I can go on and get a few more goals and play in as many games as possible. Obviously, I can make an impact if I come off the bench, but I really want to be playing over the 90 minutes.

'I have scored six goals in six games now and most of

those have been from starting games, so hopefully I can keep that run going. I'm feeling as good as I ever did.

'I don't think as a striker that you can doubt yourself. You're a hero one minute if you score and then you're the villain. If you haven't got confidence in your ability, there's no way you can play the role. I've had joy in the past against South American teams and hopefully I can get some joy in the next game.

'I don't think Ecuador will have come across my type of player before and that will definitely help me. Their goalkeeper isn't the biggest of chaps so that's something that works in my favour, too. Michael Owen is a big void to fill, but I don't know if I would say replacing him would be daunting for me. It's a shame we have lost him, but I'm confident in my ability and I believe I can do a good job. Geoff Hurst took his chance in 1966 and I'd love to emulate that.

'It's the kind of thing you dream about as a kid and it's a similar situation in that injuries have forced my way into the team. At the start of the tournament Wayne and Michael were first choice, but with them both having problems I've had more of a chance. Hopefully I have done enough.

'I hope I'm taken seriously now, and six goals in six games hasn't done me any harm. I've proved that, if I do miss, I can score later in the game. Name me a striker who doesn't miss chances. You've got to keep putting yourself in that position and I'll carry on doing that.'

And goalkeeper Robinson also backed Crouch and Rooney to keep England on track for the final in Berlin. He told the media ranks, 'I thought Wazza and Crouchy did very well together up front [against Sweden] and it looks as if that is what we will go with for the rest of the tournament.

'To lose a player of Michael's quality is bad for the team and the squad. The loss of a striker is going to be bad for any squad. But Wazza and Crouchy are playing well at the moment and we should be all right.'

England certainly could not have wished for a better draw than to face Ecuador in the last 16. Although the South Americans had performed well in the group stages, Germany had shown up their defensive weaknesses by defeating them 3–0 in their final first-round match.

They were widely regarded as being the weakest South American nation to have qualified for the finals and, having already beaten Paraguay in the group stages, England could rightly approach the game with confidence, despite the fact that they would have been concerned by their own level of performance so far.

But as they approached the Ecuador game, Beckham insisted that he and the rest of the team had to seize their opportunity to make their mark on the biggest stage of all.

Before the second-round clash, he said, 'Chances don't come as good as this too often. You look at what this competition is all about: we're an English team playing in Europe and the weather for the majority of the time has been great for us. Everything is right.

'In four years' time it [the World Cup] is in South Africa, four years after that maybe Australia or South America and we're talking different climates. So these opportunities won't come around often and we don't want to waste it. It's up to us to take this chance now.

'We're not kidding ourselves. We've lost players and we

have had situations that have not gone right for us but, as a team, we are right. The togetherness couldn't be any stronger than it is. We are so positive as a team. I have never been in a team that is so positive about going into a competition and going into games.

'We've still got that – that's not changed. People maybe have been negative towards the performances so far, but the team's morale and togetherness has not changed the whole way through this tournament.

'We're ready for Ecuador. I think they will provide a dangerous attacking threat because technically they are very, very good. They have quite a few big players – tall, strong players – and it's going to be a tough game for us.

'But we have to be confident. When we play our football, we become a very attractive team to watch, a very good team and a dangerous team.'

And one man who was hopeful that England would play to their full potential and show off their footballing ability was Crouch, who had been stung by criticism in some quarters that England had resorted to long punts upfield during the tournament to take advantage of his height advantage.

He insisted, 'I totally resent that. It's very frustrating to hear that, because I'm in the team, we're going to play long ball. Yes, it's an option we can use, but certainly not an option we want to use all the time. I think you can see that when I'm in the team. Against Sweden we didn't play any long balls. Most of the passing was to feet and that's the best way for us to play.

'I prefer to play the right way. That's the way I was brought up, playing football on the floor. In international football you can't just knock high balls in. You've got to be more cute than that. We've got a lot more talent and a lot more belief in our own ability than that.'

Perhaps predictably, given what had gone before, England struggled to impose their own game on a resilient Ecuador side. Although they enjoyed the majority of possession in the first half, they were unable to muster a clear chance and had to be content with a 0–0 scoreline at the break.

Once again, just as had been the case against Trinidad and Sweden, they would have to produce in the second half, something they had often failed to do under Eriksson. Indeed, Crouch's header in the 83rd minute against Trinidad was the first second-half goal England had scored in the World Cup finals since 1998.

And four years previously against Brazil in Japan, it was their lamentable second-half display that led to their exit at the quarter-final stage. They simply could not afford a repeat of that against Ecuador.

Fortunately, when they needed him most, Beckham produced a moment of brilliance to settle the contest and take England into the quarter-finals for the ninth time. His curling free-kick on the hour mark proved the difference between the two sides, and with it he became the first England player to score at three World Cup finals, having netted against Colombia in 1998 and having fired home the decisive penalty against Argentina four years later.

This goal may not have had the drama of that spot-kick, but it was no less important as England assured themselves of a place in the last eight. Maybe, just maybe, it would be England's year. After all, don't they say that a mark of a good team is to win even when they are not playing well?

Eriksson was delighted to be in the last eight again and promised the best was yet to come. He said, 'We are very happy. We are through to the quarter-finals of the World Cup again and I hope that we have a better result in the quarter-final than we did in the last one.

'We are into the quarter-finals and we still haven't performed as well as we can do, but I am sure that will come later.'

The quarter-final draw paired England with Portugal, and a repeat of the last-eight clash at Euro 2004 that England lost on yet another heartbreaking penalty shoot-out.

Crouch insisted there would be no repeat of that misery this time. He said, 'We have been practising every day. We know there is a chance that it could come down to a shoot-out.'

And he promised that, if it did come down to spot-kicks, there would be no repeat of his attempted chip that had gone so badly wrong in the warm-up game against Jamaica. He added, 'I let myself down at Old Trafford. I'm sure I won't be taking penalties like that out here, but whether the manager wants me to take a penalty or not is a different story.'

For Eriksson and England, the game marked a third successive quarter-final against 'Big Phil' Scolari, with the Three Lions having been beaten on both the previous two occasions.

In 2002, Scolari steered his native Brazil past England

in the last eight and on to win the tournament, while at Euro 2004 he masterminded the host's run to the final – where they lost to Greece – defeating England in that last-eight shoot-out along the way.

And the game was given added significance, of course, by the fact that the FA had approached Scolari with a view to him succeeding Eriksson as England head coach after the finals. He turned the opportunity down – although the FA later claimed the job was never formally offered to him – and Steve McClaren was promoted from within.

Not that Eriksson was suffering from any kind of inferiority complex as he approached the match in Gelsenkirchen.

He said, 'This game is important for both us and Portugal. I think we will win, but their manager will think his team will win. There are a lot of good managers at this World Cup, and maybe Scolari is the best – but maybe not.

'We have had an extra week's rest since the end of the domestic season than we did two and four years ago, so that could be very important in this game.

'We lost the game against Portugal on penalties in Euro 2004, but we have a better squad now than we did then, and it will be a special feeling to reach the semi-finals of the World Cup.'

And there was no doubt that England's players were looking for revenge for that last-eight defeat of two years previously. Midfielder Owen Hargreaves told the media, 'In football there is such a fine line between winning and losing. Even when you look at that game in Euro 2004, there were so many highs and lows and obviously with penalties it can go either way.

'That time it didn't swing our way and we're looking to put things right. This is a different tournament, two years on. It's difficult when you prepare for a big tournament, put in all that effort and time in qualifying and then the game is suddenly decided like that. And you realise you're going home the next day.

'It was so disappointing and it's very hard to describe how it is. It is very difficult. Football can be very harsh at times. We could very easily have gone on to the semi-final that time, but we didn't.

'But when you've been in those situations, realised that it's that close and such a fine line, you realise that it comes down to the tiny little details. You have to decide them for yourself to move on. That's what we want to do this time.

'We're very positive. We have a very talented group of individuals and one of the most successful managers in football. I think we have all the positives going into the game. We're determined to win this time.'

Determined they may have been, but once again the footballing gods were not on England's side. And once again it was Rooney who was at the centre of the action.

Eriksson had decided to leave Crouch out of the starting line-up against the Portuguese, choosing to play a 4-5-1 formation with Rooney as the lone striker. Many pundits predicted the system would fail with Rooney growing frustrated at fighting to retain possession on his own. That is exactly how it transpired.

Two years previously, Rooney had limped off injured against Portugal in the quarter-final, and with him went England's best chance of success, as they had been totally dominant up to that point in the game. On this occasion, however, it was the referee who deemed that the Manchester United striker would not finish the contest.

With just over an hour played, Rooney was sent off for stamping on Ricardo Carvalho as he lay on the ground with the ball between his legs. It looked a harsh decision, but Rooney's cause wasn't helped by his Old Trafford colleague Cristiano Ronaldo racing towards the referee gesturing for the England ace to be dismissed.

Rooney reacted angrily by shoving the Portuguese wide man in the chest but, when the melee calmed down, it was the England man who was ushered towards the tunnel, and once more in a crucial World Cup game, with echoes of Beckham against Argentina eight years previously in France, England were down to ten men.

Just as on that occasion in France, however, the expulsion of a team-mate seemed to galvanise England and they performed heroics to keep Portugal at bay for the remaining half an hour of normal time and throughout the 30 minutes of extra-time.

All of which meant, predictably, that England's fate in a major tournament would once again be decided by penalties. And, amid bitter memories of Italia '90 and Euro '96 against the Germans, of France '98 against Argentina and of Euro 2004 against Portugal, the Three Lions came off second best once again.

Lampard, Gerrard and Carragher all saw their spot-kicks saved by goalkeeper Ricardo, with only Hargreaves succeeding with his effort, while Simao Sabrossa, Helder Postiga and Cristiano Ronaldo – rubbing salt into the wound he had opened up earlier in the contest – all beat Robinson to clinch a 3–1 shoot-out victory for the Portuguese.

It was a bitter pill for England to swallow and, afterwards, several of the players slumped to the turf in tears. But the stark reality was that the so-called 'golden generation' had failed to deliver when it mattered most and, despite the gallant sense of their ultimate failure against Portugal, the fact remained that they had grossly underperformed in Germany.

Eriksson said, 'I am very sorry for the players and for the fans. I've been convinced all along that this team had the potential to win the World Cup, but we were a little bit unlucky. I must say they fought enormously when it was ten against eleven. We held the game up very well and lost on penalties again and I'm really sorry about that.

'We practised penalties so much, I really don't know what more we could have done about it. We have practised for the last four or five weeks. They have been very good in training, but when it comes to the final stages we miss them.

'I don't think we deserved to lose and I think the boys deserved better. But we lost the game and went out of the tournament and that hurts incredibly. We gave a good performance, but we're out and that's very painful. I'm sorry for the players and very sorry for the fans, who have been fantastic, that we couldn't give them a final.'

It was not the way Eriksson would have wanted to end his tenure as England head coach, but he insisted that his number two, Steve McClaren, was inheriting an excellent squad and one that would only get better.

He added, 'We had a very good chance to win the

World Cup but we didn't take it. But I think England will have opportunities in the future because they have a lot of good young players coming through: Walcott, Lennon, Downing, they will be even better in two years' time, so I think the future is very good.

'I have enjoyed every minute of the job and I have been very proud to have it.'

While it may not have been the happy ending Eriksson had wished for, neither was it the way Crouch would have wanted the tournament to end for him – consigned to the bench for the biggest game of the competition and thrown into the fray as a substitute for Joe Cole to fight for scraps and try desperately to hold the ball up in a solo effort to give England's beleaguered rearguard a breather.

He later admitted to *FourFourTwo* magazine, 'Personally, I think 4-4-2 would have been better [against Portugal], but obviously the manager made his decision. Rooney's a top-class player and he can play that role as well as anyone, but he'll tell you himself he would have liked to have played with a partner.'

Crouch confessed that his immediate thoughts on seeing the red card brandished in Rooney's face was not that the team were in trouble, but that he was likely to be called into immediate action.

He said, 'That's exactly what I thought, "I'm on." Obviously people at home were devastated, but as a player you've got to prepare and stay focused. As soon as he went off, I was warming up because I knew there was a pretty good chance that I'd come on. You've got to get your head right.'

Had the shoot-out against Portugal gone to sudden death, Crouch was seventh in line to take a penalty. How was he feeling at the time? 'I was buzzing, I was excited, I would have liked to have taken one. Apart from the horrific one against Jamaica, I'm all right at taking penalties.'

Perhaps if more of England's players could say the same, particularly in big international tournaments, the recent history of the Three Lions would have been very, very different.

CHAPTER 7

BACK WITH THE REDS

After ending his first season at Liverpool with an FA Cup winners' medal, third place in the Premiership and 12 goals to his credit, Crouch had every reason to feel pleased with himself.

Then, having proved to the doubters both before and during the World Cup that he could score goals at international level, he had every reason to approach the new season with confidence.

What he probably didn't expect was for his manager to declare publicly that he had to prove himself all over again. Whether Rafael Benitez meant the threat as a gentle kick up the backside or as something more sinister, only he knows.

But, having signed Craig Bellamy from Blackburn during the summer and lined up a deal for Feyenoord's Dutch international striker Dirk Kuyt, he then left Crouch on the bench for Liverpool's Champions League win over Maccabi Haifa in the first leg of their qualifying clash before telling him he had to do it all over again to establish himself on Merseyside.

Benitez told a news conference after the match, 'This year, Peter is more mature and he needs to understand what it means to be a Liverpool player. He needs to improve in some areas and keep doing the things he has done well. You cannot stop improving.

'He needs to know how important it is to score goals, to make assists and to work hard for a club like this. I think he's going about things the right way.

'People were talking before he signed that he wasn't good for us. But after a while he was in the squad with the national team and now people know how good he is. But he cannot think that is enough. He now needs to continue improving, as he has a lot of potential and possibilities.'

Crouch was back in the team three days later for the first real test of the season – the FA Community Shield against Chelsea at the Millennium Stadium.

The traditional curtain-raiser to the Premiership is often little more than a glorified pre-season friendly, but, given the bitter rivalry that had developed between the two sides over the past two seasons, there was always going to be an edge to proceedings in Cardiff.

And Liverpool were determined to draw first blood and set down a marker for the rest of the season, as well as claiming another piece of silverware.

Benitez said, 'I would say this game is an important preparation match. Whenever you play against a good team, and you're both trying to win a trophy, it is always important. Of course, it is not the most important game we will play, but we both still want to win.

'It can help in terms of confidence, but our main aim is to keep on progressing through the season, not just in this match. I see this game as an opportunity for us to improve our quality and our fitness. It's difficult to say any team will get a big advantage for the season by winning the game.

'I don't know if either team will be at their best at this stage. Both of us had a lot of players away for the World Cup who have not trained as much as the others. We will pick a side I believe is strongest for the day, considering the fitness of the players and the important games we have to follow.'

Chelsea boss Jose Mourinho, meanwhile, got his retaliation in first by claiming that Liverpool had the upper hand because they had already played a competitive match, against Maccabi Haifa, while his side had not.

But, whatever the respective managers had to say, Liverpool got the win they wanted courtesy of goals from Riise and Crouch, although, when the Norwegian struck in only the ninth minute, the Reds' supporters must have recalled his stunning first-minute volley against Chelsea on the same ground in the Carling Cup final of 2005. On that occasion, Mourinho's men recovered to win 3–2 and claim his first trophy in England, while denying Benitez his.

And when Andriy Shevchenko equalised for the Blues – his first goal for them following his £30 million summer move from AC Milan – the red half of the ground must have feared a repeat of that comeback.

They need not have worried, though, because Crouch was on hand ten minutes from time to head home Bellamy's cross to give the Anfield fans the win they would cherish. And, having waited so long to get off the mark the previous season, it must have come as a huge relief to Crouch to have opened his account in his first start of the new campaign.

And he was delighted to return to Cardiff and pick up another winners' medal just a couple of months after that memorable FA Cup triumph. He told journalists after the game, 'I want to win things and this is a good start to the season. We hope it is going to be a good season. People say it's not important to win the Community Shield, but you can see that the fans and the players see it is important.'

Benitez was equally happy and was full of praise for his players, and Crouch in particular. He said, 'I am happy with the performance of my team and the work-rate of the players was fantastic. It is always important to win against the top sides and always important when you win a trophy. It is very good for the confidence of the team.

'We have a better team and a better squad than last season and we have more pace and energy in the attack. I was really pleased to see Crouch score and it is really important for him, because scoring goals gives strikers more confidence.'

And Crouch took that confidence with him when he joined up with the England squad for McClaren's first game in charge of the Three Lions, a friendly against Greece at Old Trafford. And it would be fair to say that things could not have gone better for either McClaren or Crouch.

It's almost certain that Crouch would not have started

against the Greeks, with McClaren making clear his intention to award Dean Ashton his first cap. But, when the West Ham star tragically broke an ankle in training just a couple of days before the match, the door was opened for Crouch.

And he barged through it and took his chance to impress with both hands.

England were already cruising towards victory against a woeful Greek side, looking a pale imitation of the team that had so famously triumphed at Euro 2004, thanks to goals from new captain John Terry and his Chelsea team-mate Lampard, when Crouch took centre stage.

He grabbed his first goal from close range in the 36th minute after good work from Lampard and Stewart Downing and, six minutes later, he headed home his second – and England's fourth – from Downing's cross.

It was the perfect start to McClaren's reign – the best by an England manager for 60 years – and provided further proof that Crouch was a threat to be reckoned with at the top level. Indeed, his double at Old Trafford took his tally to eight goals in just 12 internationals, some record by anyone's standards.

Not surprisingly, McClaren could not have been happier with his first game in charge. 'I'm absolutely delighted,' he said. 'Particularly with the first-half performance when the players did everything we asked of them. We played with a lot of freedom and lost any fear after the first goal went in, and some of the performances were outstanding.'

It was indeed an impressive beginning to a new era for England and, while the manager was pleased with his players, they too were equally keen on what they had seen from their new boss after he stepped out of Eriksson's shadow.

Crouch told reporters, 'It has been good under the new management team. Terry Venables and Steve Round are very much hands-on and get involved in training. We have all enjoyed it and hopefully we will see a bit more when we join up for the next games.

'Everyone has got a bit to say and there is input from everywhere. Steve McClaren and Terry Venables are running it and we have enjoyed every minute.

'Steve [McClaren] doesn't want the players to be stationary and wants us to move around. At times you saw Steven Gerrard come in from midfield [against Greece] and I would go wide.

'He doesn't want us to be static and I think it worked well against Greece. We have worked on it quite a bit in training. If one player moves out of an area then another player fills in for them. If you feel comfortable doing that in international football, then it works well.

'The result could not have gone much better for us. We had been working all week on how we were going to play and it clicked straight away. I thought everyone did well throughout the team and it was a joy to play out there because we all felt comfortable and passed the ball around really well.'

Crouch's two-goal display and the adulation he received from the crowd were a far cry from that October night just ten months previously when he had been heckled and abused against Poland.

He admitted, 'Sometimes I think back to when I was

getting some stick, but I like to think I have won the fans over. It was never an issue with my team-mates or manager. I always had the confidence in my ability and hopefully that is showing now.

'I like to think people are seeing that and hopefully I can move on from here and this is just the start for me. I want to be involved in the next European Championship and the World Cup.

'The manager at Liverpool is the first to tell you if you have done well and what you could have done better. I'm sure I will go into his office [after the Greece game] and he will tell me where I can improve again. That is the type of person he is, because he only wants me to improve and get better.'

Indeed, Crouch returned to Anfield after his two-goal heroics for his country not even sure whether he would be in the team for Liverpool's first Premiership game of the season at Bramall Lane, the home of newly promoted Sheffield United. In fact, he wasn't.

Instead, he had to be content with a place on the bench as Benitez started with Bellamy and Fowler in attack, and it was Fowler who netted the Reds' equaliser from the penalty spot to earn them a 1–1 draw.

Having started with Bellamy as the lone front man against Maccabi Haifa in the first leg of their Champions League qualifier, and then paired Crouch and Luis Garcia against Chelsea in Cardiff, it was clear when Benitez named his third different attacking formation in as many matches to face Sheffield United that he was planning to rotate his squad in the months ahead.

Crouch was back in the starting line-up for the next

match, though, the return of the Champions League qualifier against Maccabi Haifa which, because of the political tension in Israel, was to be held on neutral territory in Kiev.

Again he was partnered by Luis Garcia and, with the game delicately balanced at just 2–1 in favour of the Anfield side following the first meeting on Merseyside, they knew it was not going to be easy to progress and book their place in the lucrative group stages.

Indeed, on the eve of the match goalkeeper Reina had warned, 'Maccabi showed at Anfield they are fast and dangerous in attack and organised in defence. This will be a complicated second leg for Liverpool.'

'It wasn't a good start to our campaign, conceding a goal to Haifa at home,' the Spaniard continued on the club's website. 'We all know the importance of scoring away goals in Europe. We had a lot of possession in the first match, but it doesn't count for anything.

'In football you can control games, but you must make it count with goals. The key for us will be to score in Kiev. Rafa Benitez has described this match as the most important game of our season and I agree. It has to be, "We have to qualify for the next round of the Champions League" – it is as simple as that.'

Reina highlighted the importance of finding the back of the net in the Ukraine and Crouch duly obliged, netting his fourth goal in as many games as he made a blistering start to the new season. Although Roberto Colautti equalised on the night for the Israelis, Liverpool held on to seal a 3–2 aggregate victory.

Benitez admitted, 'It was a difficult game, but it's good

to have qualified. I am really happy. It's not been easy to start pre-season without some players and our results in pre-season were not the best, so it's always a relief to come through a tie like this. I am sure that once the next international break is out of the way you will see the team improve.

'In the first half we had a lot of clear chances, but their goalkeeper was fantastic. In my opinion, he was man of the match. We had some problems towards the end defensively, but that is normal when a team is chasing the game. In these situations we need to score again to kill the game.'

Crouch confessed that Liverpool had been forced to 'dig deep' to secure their passage to the group stage, and he stressed that he was enjoying the service he was receiving from the club's two new wingers, Jermaine Pennant and Mark Gonzalez.

'It was a difficult game, they were no mugs at all and they proved that. It was not the prettiest of wins, but it got us through,' he told liverpoolfc.tv. 'It's good for someone like myself to have two wingers and it's a case of getting in the box. There's always going to be competition at a big club, but hopefully I can thrive on that.'

With the games coming thick and fast, there was little time for Liverpool to reflect on their success in Kiev. Instead, they were straight back to England in readiness for a Saturday-lunchtime kick-off against West Ham.

Having served up a six-goal thriller at the Millennium Stadium just a few months earlier, it was too much for the neutrals to expect another classic, but the game did provide two stunning moments to earn Liverpool the three points.

After the Hammers had taken the lead courtesy of Bobby Zamora's sliced attempted cross that completely deceived Reina and beat him at the near post, Liverpool took control and were in front before half-time.

Firstly, Danish centre-back Daniel Agger scored his first goal for the club with an unstoppable 30-yard left-foot drive on 42 minutes and then, on the stroke of half-time, Crouch turned the game on its head with a second goal.

He took Luis Garcia's clever pass in his stride before demonstrating once again that he has terrific skills and ability with the ball at his feet by dancing around goalkeeper Roy Carroll and sliding the ball into a gaping net.

They were two superb goals and a fitting way for the team to mark the occasion of the 100th anniversary of their Anfield stadium.

His goal made it five in five games for Crouch for club and country in a terrific start to the season he could surely only have dreamed about. And, with the Euro 2008 qualification campaign about to start, he could not have picked a better time to hit such a rich vein of form.

With Rooney suspended for the double header against Andorra at home and Macedonia away after his World Cup red card, there was never any doubt that Crouch would be in the starting XI. And, once again, he did not disappoint.

The part-time Andorrans were never expected to be a match for England and, although the players and management trotted out the usual platitudes in the build-up to the game at Old Trafford, England fans were expecting a landslide victory. And that is exactly what they got.

Crouch started up front alongside Jermain Defoe, so keen to prove that Eriksson had made a mistake by leaving him out of the World Cup squad for the finals in Germany, and the pair performed superbly together.

The Liverpool star got the ball rolling as early as the fifth minute, with an excellent left-foot shot from Ashley Cole's neat pass, and from there the floodgates opened.

Gerrard made it 2–0 in the 13th minute with a ferocious right-foot drive, and he then turned provider 25 minutes later, crossing from the right for Defoe to smash home a tidy left-foot volley.

Defoe added his second of the afternoon two minutes after half-time, before Crouch made it 5–0 to complete the rout when he headed home substitute Aaron Lennon's pinpoint cross.

It was another convincing win for the Three Lions, coming on the back of the 4–0 thrashing of Greece, and meant that McClaren's first two games in charge had both ended in confident victories, with nine goals scored and none conceded.

The England head coach was delighted with the display and felt it set the squad up nicely for the trip to Macedonia in midweek. He said, 'We handled this game very well and the players did everything that was asked of them. We controlled the tempo of the game, we stayed patient, never got frustrated and scored our goals at the right time and maybe could have had even more.

'We did well, but Macedonia away is another game and will be a different test. It will be a challenge and a test of character to see if we can go away from home and control a game and get the win. It will be difficult, but the way we performed last time against Greece and then with this result, we can go to Macedonia full of confidence.'

McClaren also had special words of praise for Crouch, who took his international goals' tally to ten in just 13 appearances. In fact, all ten goals had come in his last nine matches, with seven of them coming in just three appearances at Old Trafford.

The England head coach said, 'His goal-scoring record is phenomenal. He is such a handful for defenders. Is he un-droppable? No one is un-droppable, but when he is scoring at that rate you need him in your team.

'What I like most about him is that he is a team player. We analyse the stats and it is consistently Peter Crouch who runs the most out of anybody on the team. You would think it would be a midfield player, but it's Crouch every time.

'He runs about 13 kilometres in a game. The average is between 12 and 12½ for a midfield player and he is consistently above that. I've seen Crouch do over 14 kilometres, which is amazing for a striker.

'He's disciplined to do a job, he's got a great touch with his back to goal, brings others into play and you can give him the ball and trust him with it. He's also an aerial threat and he's an outlet for us, so he's got many, many qualities.

'With those long legs, he couldn't be the fastest, but he's effective in other ways. Teddy Sheringham wasn't quick but he was very, very effective. Peter is good enough to score against top defenders.

'If you have confidence, you always seem to be in the right spot at the right time and that's what he's doing.'

Crouch's scoring streak even had Gerrard telling him after the game that he was on course to beat Sir Bobby Charlton's 49-goal England record, but, while that milestone may still have been some way off, he was nonetheless relishing his current success for his country, particularly at the home of Liverpool's bitter north-west rivals.

He told the media after the Andorra win, 'I love playing at Old Trafford, and for England. I was disappointed not to have got a hat-trick, but pleased we got the result. I have to score to stay in the team because of the competition.

'There are two big players to come back into the game in Wayne Rooney and Michael Owen, so I just have to express myself when I get the chance. Hopefully I can do enough to give the manager something to think about.

'Steven Gerrard told me in the changing room that I could be chasing Bobby Charlton's record if I keep up this goal-scoring run. I have just got to keep on going and I am enjoying myself at the moment. I just hope I can get more chances to score goals for England.

'We are a creative side and it is great to play in a team like this that creates so many good chances. Thankfully I managed to score a couple of goals as well. There have been times when I have not scored, but at the moment I am scoring goals and I am really enjoying my football.'

'I do love playing at Old Trafford and just love playing for England. We have got an attacking team and I always know that I am going to get chances.'

And, even though he was prepared to accept that when Rooney and Owen were available he would almost certainly revert back to being part of McClaren's Plan B, he said, 'At least I'm in a plan!'

He added, 'Everybody wants to be part of Plan A, and hopefully I can convince people I'm worthy of a start. If you ask the manager, I am part of his Plan A because I'm playing in his starting team at the moment.'

The confident win over Andorra was an excellent start to the Euro 2008 qualifying campaign, but McClaren was taking nothing for granted as he contemplated a tricky trip to Macedonia for the second game.

The Macedonians had given England a stern test in the qualifying tournament for the 2004 European Championship, drawing 2–2 at Southampton's St Mary's Stadium and then taking the lead in their home match, before goals from Rooney and Beckham earned England a hard-fought 2–1 win.

The England head coach said, 'We've got this qualifying campaign off to a good start, but people are saying this will be an easy game. My message is: don't underestimate Macedonia. They have won their last three away games and drew twice with Holland in the World Cup qualifiers.

'They have an experienced manager and they are the home side, but, if we take all these ingredients into account, don't underestimate them and play to our potential, we should get the points.

'They surprised us at St Mary's in 2002 because they are very quick and good on the break. It was a great atmosphere in Skopje in 2003 and I expect that again.'

McClaren made just one change from the side that had thrashed Andorra, with Rio Ferdinand, having recovered from a knock, replacing his Manchester United teammate Wes Brown in the centre of defence.

But, as McClaren had warned, it certainly wasn't the

stroll in the park England had enjoyed against the Andorrans a few days previously, and they had to battle hard and show great resolve to claim all three points.

But when the winning goal came, just a minute after half-time, it was one of genuine quality. Lampard did well to cut the ball back from the right and Crouch, with his back to goal and falling away from the target, produced a stunning overhead volley that bounced down off the crossbar and over the line.

It was a magnificent finish and provided further proof, if any were needed at this stage, that Crouch was a player of great skill and technique. There are many Premiership strikers who fit the more traditional 'photo-fit' of a top-class forward who would have been proud of such a finish.

It was his 11th goal in his last ten internationals, making him probably the world's hottest striker at the time, and ensured that England had started their Euro 2008 campaign with two priceless wins and six points out of six.

'He [Crouch] is such a threat,' said McClaren afterwards. 'He leads the line well. He took a lot of stick tonight and was unfortunate with decisions from the referee all game, but he stuck at his task and he took his opportunity very well.

'I actually missed it [the goal]. I had just finished my half-time team talk and I was thinking about the second half. I have done it in the past and it worked – and it's worked again! But I saw the goal on the television monitor and it was a very good goal.'

Crouch's incredible scoring ratio in the early part of his England career meant he had a better games-per-goals return at this stage than legends such as Alan Shearer and Gary Lineker, and he could not have been happier.

He told thefa.com, 'It [Macedonia] is a difficult place to come, a hostile atmosphere and we knew they were a good team. They made it difficult for us and the pitch is not what we are used to. But the team showed good character and resilience and we defended well and we've come out with the right result.

'I've been told it [the ball] was over the line. I just had my back to goal and swivelled, so I didn't see it go over the line. It took an age for the referee to give it, but thankfully he did.'

And that strike prompted Phil Neville to hail Crouch as one of the world's best forwards. The Everton star said of his Merseyside rival, 'I think in terms of international football, Crouchy is one of the most in-form strikers in world football at the moment. His goal-scoring record is phenomenal.'

Neville continued in an interview with the Press Association, 'People go on about his height, but his technical ability is second to none of any striker I know. He is a real threat when these games come along. Hopefully he keeps scoring. He has been superb.'

That goal in Macedonia capped a remarkable few weeks for Crouch and took his combined tally for club and country to eight in just seven matches. Little wonder that his colleagues were queuing up to pay tribute to him.

And Anfield boss Benitez was quick to add his own words of tribute. He told the club's website, 'I'm really happy for him but also worried because people will start talking really well about him, and as a manager you must give him confidence, but also say to him, "Be careful", because every week things can change, so you need to keep going.

'I think he's scoring in the right ways, but he has to be careful, because, when people start talking really well about you, you can think, "OK, I am better than I really am," and then you stop working as hard as before. But I know that he is clever and he will continue going forward and working hard.'

But while everything in the international garden was rosy, Liverpool's start to the Premiership season had not been quite so straightforward. Everyone at Anfield had talked before the campaign kicked off of the need to make a fast start and to ensure they did not allow Chelsea to open up a gap, as had been the case in the previous two years.

Four points from their first two games was a decent return, but they would have hoped for maximum points from an away trip to Sheffield United and a home game against West Ham, particularly with their next two domestic matches being trips to local rivals Everton and fierce enemies Chelsea, either side of a European date in Holland with PSV Eindhoven.

And, if there was some concern about their start to the campaign before the Everton match, those fears were exacerbated on a day the red half of Merseyside will want to forget quickly.

Before the game, manager Benitez had stressed the need for his players to be mentally ready for the challenge ahead. 'I hope they will be ready because, like I said before, they have experience in these kinds of games and they know how important and exciting the game will be. It will be more mental than physical. It will be a tough game, pretty physical with a lot of second balls and a lot of tackles.

'If you ask me whether I prefer to win a derby match or win trophies I will always say that to win a trophy is the most important thing, but if we can win a derby and a trophy then it makes it better,' he told the club's website.

'I like to win the derby because it makes our supporters happy and you can see them smiling in the town. The derby is a very important game for us and I know how special it is for the supporters.'

But, after seeing his side go down 3–0 to goals from Tim Cahill and Andy Johnson (two), he was left to bemoan the defensive frailties that cost his side any chance of taking something from the game.

Benitez said, 'We made a lot of mistakes, too many mistakes, and our defending was really poor. Last season we had a lot of clean sheets so we need to analyse why we are conceding goals so easily.

'I thought we were too nice at times and put ourselves under pressure. Someone said to me we had 21 shots at goal but that counts for nothing if you don't take your chances. It is a very disappointing day for us for sure.'

The good news for Liverpool was that, at this early stage of the season, there was no time to dwell on the defeat at Everton as they were straight off to Holland to take on Eindhoven in their first Champions League group game.

And Benitez was determined that they would put the derby setback behind them. He said, 'If you want to change things you need to play again and to win. It's as simple as that. I hope I don't see a lot of mistakes [against PSV] – at least not in our team. Always as a manager you think you can improve and I think you will see a lot of positive things.'

The Spaniard continued his rotation policy, making six changes from the game at Goodison Park, with Crouch one of the players relegated to the bench, along with the likes of captain Steven Gerrard and defensive stalwart Sami Hyypia. Crouch wasn't called upon as Liverpool got their European Cup campaign off to a credible start with a 0–0 draw.

Benitez said afterwards, 'The team worked really, really hard. You could see the midfielders and the strikers supporting the defenders. It was our idea to keep a clean sheet and to go forward, and we had enough clear chances to maybe have scored one goal.

'At the end we have one point, but I think we created enough chances to win. But after playing seven games in 21 days, with a lot of players coming back from international duty, I think we showed we can play and it's not bad.

'In the Champions League you never know but, with the experience and quality of PSV, if you can draw here and win at home you are in a good position – but you need to win at home.'

The Spaniard was also forced to answer questions from the media about the constant shuffling of his playing personnel, but he insisted he knew what he was doing. He claimed, 'I have explained many, many times that we can't play every game at 100 per cent.

'We played against Everton, a difficult game, and decided to change. We have a good squad and we can use different players. We have more options in every game and I always talk about a long race. I don't talk about one game and two games.'

But, while there were positives for Benitez and Liverpool to draw upon, not least their first clean sheet of the season, there were still question marks over the team when they returned to domestic action in their biggest game of the season so far – away to Chelsea.

Benitez's side had proved to be a constant thorn in the side of the champions in cup competitions, but had been unable to repeat that form in league encounters. In fact, Chelsea had beaten Liverpool on all four occasions they had met in the Premiership since the Spaniard's arrival at Anfield in the summer of 2004.

And a well-documented feud between the two managers did nothing to quell the sense of tension as the game approached. And with Liverpool having taken only four points from their first three matches, there was a genuine need for them to get something at Stamford Bridge to prevent Chelsea from widening the gap at the top.

Not that Benitez was prepared to admit that the game would have any ultimate bearing on the Premiership title race. He said, 'I'm surprised so many people are saying, if we lose, the title will be impossible. I know, if that happens, people will say we have no chance, and if we win they'll say we are in a race. It's still too early for this.

'Last year we won one of the first six league games, but finished the season with 82 points and came third. This time, I wouldn't be surprised if a team with 75 points finished first. The Premiership is much stronger this year and a lot of clubs have improved. All the top clubs may have more problems.

'Last season, Chelsea won many games, but I don't think it will be so easy for anyone this time. More teams will beat each other, and already some of the top teams are having difficulties at the start of the season.

'I promise you I am not looking at the table now, after just three games. The time to analyse the table is in another two months, and then you will see how the team is progressing.

'You never know whether it's a good or bad time to play them [Chelsea] until after the game. It's never easy playing two games in a week, but at least we've been able to train with the players, talk to them and analyse things. That's better than our preparations for last week.

'Maybe after the result at PSV, our confidence is better. It's a big test for us, but we can be sure the motivation of the players going into the game is really good. These are the games the players like to play in. They want to show we are strong and improve the results against the top sides in the Premiership.

'Last season we had problems in the league games against them and we want to do much better.

'We've done a good job against them in the cups and now we want to do the same in the Premiership. The cup is always different. Both teams know there can be no draw, and it makes a difference to the tactical approach. It's a different type of game in the Premiership, with different problems.'

Unfortunately for Crouch, he found himself among the substitutes again as Benitez stuck with the front pairing that had performed admirably in Eindhoven, Bellamy and Kuyt. And Liverpool certainly enjoyed plenty of possession and had chances to win the game, but once more they left Stamford Bridge empty-handed.

Kuyt struck the crossbar with a thunderous drive that left Chelsea goalkeeper Petr Cech helpless, and the Reds certainly had legitimate claims for a penalty when Gerrard appeared to be bundled over by his England colleague Lampard. As it was, however, Chelsea sneaked the win, despite playing for much of the second half with only ten men after German midfield star Michael Ballack was sent off for stamping on Momo Sissoko.

The only consolation for Liverpool, if it was one at all, was that they were beaten by a truly stunning strike from Didier Drogba, with the big Ivory Coast striker controlling the ball on his chest before, in one movement, swivelling and striking a magnificent left-foot volley from the edge of the penalty area that gave Reina absolutely no chance.

Benitez himself felt his side had been unfortunate. He said, 'I think we deserved more from the game. In the first half we created clear chances through Kuyt and Gerrard, but one player won the game for Chelsea with a fantastic goal.

'We started the second half creating more chances and getting into good positions. The push on Gerrard by Lampard was a clear penalty, but we cannot change these things now.

'We are improving and if we keep playing like this we will score goals. It's clear that we need more points, but it's only the beginning of the season and it's a long race. We need to get going.'

That defeat, though, left Liverpool eight points behind Chelsea and Manchester United, albeit with a game in hand, but it was becoming increasingly obvious that they could ill afford too many more slip-ups in the league.

Still, however, there was no place in the starting line-up for Crouch in the next game against Newcastle as Benitez again preferred the partnership of Bellamy and Kuyt. The Dutchman scored his first goal for the club in the 2–0 win to vindicate that decision, and once again Crouch had to satisfy himself with a brief cameo from the bench.

The striker found himself in a strange paradox – first choice for his country and, in his international manager's words virtually 'un-droppable', yet relegated to the bench for his club, and a club that was struggling for goals at that.

But Benitez would not be swayed. He insisted, 'For me, rotation is really important if you want to compete in three or four competitions. Sometimes it's better to play a big name who is 80 per cent fit than a player who is 100 per cent, but sometimes it is not.

'Crouch knows me, he knows I like to put players under pressure. If you say to him you can improve this, it shows you have confidence in him, you know he's a good player and can get better.

'If Crouch scores goals and comes here and I say, "Hey, you're the best," that's no good. I must put him under pressure and say, "Keep your feet on the ground, work harder." The players appreciate it's good for them. Sometimes they don't like it if you put them under pressure, but you're trying to improve their play.'

And the frustration continued for Crouch just three

days later when Tottenham visited Anfield. Again Bellamy and Kuyt started. Again Crouch was among the substitutes. And this time he wasn't called upon at all as Liverpool ran out comfortable 3–0 winners with goals from Gonzalez, Kuyt and Riise.

After two wins in the space of four days to revitalise their league campaign, with five goals scored and none conceded, it was beginning to look as though Crouch could find himself out of the picture for some time.

But typically of Benitez – remember, this is a man who had not picked the same side for more than 90 consecutive games – he rang the changes once more for the next match, a Champions League clash with Galatasaray, and Crouch found himself in from the start, alongside Kuyt for the first time.

Once again, however, Benitez found himself having to defend himself against accusations of tinkering, something that probably went a long way to costing previous Chelsea boss Claudio Ranieiri, who was nicknamed 'The Tinker Man', his job.

Instead of criticising the policy, though, Benitez insisted that English fans and the media had to get used to a more continental style of doing things.

He told the club's website, 'It's clear you cannot play 65 games with the same players. Talking with our English players, it's obvious they would like to play in all of the games, but, if you can win games while changing players and so keeping fresh legs until the end of the season when you can play for trophies, it's a much better situation.

'The problem is, if you make a mistake and your team selection isn't the best, then people will point to rotation if you start losing games. We all know we can't do everything perfectly, but we are always looking at the big picture and we know what we are doing is for the good of the team.

'The players understand. It's not easy when you have an important game to say they have to wait until maybe the second half before playing, but they understand I am thinking about the team and not about going against a particular player. It's all about winning games and trophies.

'If I think I need to keep some players in the team then I will do it, but if I think there are others who can come in and bring us something different then I will use them. If you want to win trophies then you always have to keep the big picture in your mind and protect the players when necessary.

'I know they all want to play, particularly in the big games, but sometimes it's important to give them a rest and make sure they are fit for the next two or three matches. If you lose a match then sometimes the next match becomes the most important. It's all about making decisions and we can do that because we see them every day in every training session.

'Don't forget, at Liverpool we won the Champions League in my first season. You can say to me we were really bad in the Premier League, particularly away from home, and I can accept that, but if you can win the Champions League then it's clear what we can achieve.'

As for Crouch, he was determined to take his chance when it came against the Turkish side. And take it he did, in some style.

It took just nine minutes for him to prove the point that

he should be starting more regularly when he neatly side-footed home Fabio Aurelio's left-wing cross to give Liverpool a great start. And five minutes later it looked as though the game was all but over when Pennant picked out Luis Garcia at the far post and the Spaniard scored with a powerful header.

But those goals merely turned out to be the hors d'oeuvres before the main course served up by Crouch seven minutes into the second half. It was then that he met Steve Finnan's perfectly flighted cross with a sensational horizontal scissors kick that sent the ball rocketing into the back of the net.

It was an extraordinary finish and almost raised the roof at the Kop end. It was also nice for Crouch to see it come off, as on the previous occasion he attempted the same skill, for England against Trinidad & Tobago in the World Cup, his shot had almost hit the corner flag!

His screamer put Liverpool 3–0 up and on their way to three important Champions League points, although they did have to withstand a nervous finish after they relaxed prematurely and allowed Umit Karan to bring the scoreline back to 3–2 with two headed goals.

Despite that defensive sloppiness, however, the Reds hung on to win and afterwards all the talk, predictably, was about Crouch's stunning goal.

He admitted to the media, 'It's the best goal I have scored for Liverpool. It's nice to get one like that at the Kop end – I don't get many. Most of the time they go over the stand when I try that.'

Benitez also hailed his striker's wonder goal, saying, 'It was a really amazing goal. We talk of the qualities of Peter

Crouch and you can see why with that goal – he is a very good player.'

Crouch knew, though, that, despite his amazing goal, he was not guaranteed a place in the team for the next game against Bolton. Having been on the bench for the four matches prior to the Galatasaray clash, he knew he could find himself there again when the team visited the Reebok Stadium.

He did admit that he was feeling a little frustrated at being left out of the side, but he was happy to accept Benitez's decisions. He continued, 'Although I scored two goals against Galatasaray, there is no telling whether I will be playing in the next game.

'I feel as though I've done well with the two goals, but the manager likes to chop and change. That's the way he works and it certainly keeps you on your toes – and he's certainly kept me on my toes.

'But he gets results and you can't go bashing down the door if he gets results. That's frustrating, because obviously as a footballer you want to be playing every game. But you've got to keep yourself ready, because you know he's going to throw you in at any time. You've got to keep sharp in training and when your chance comes you've got to take it.

'It has been frustrating and I was particularly eager to prove a point after sitting out the last few games. Hopefully I have done that, but there is no telling if I will be playing at Bolton. But I'll just keep working hard to improve and hopefully I'll continue to get my chance.

'Perhaps it's going to be even more of a challenge for me this season, but that keeps you hungry. When you haven't played a game it keeps you fresh and ready for the next one. It works, so you can't fault it.

'It is hard to get your head around it when you are sitting on the bench, especially when you haven't had that before. All you can do when you get a chance is grab it with both hands and I did that.'

Perhaps it was no surprise then, that when the team was named for the Bolton match, Crouch was again named among the substitutes. He did go on four minutes into the second half, but by then Liverpool were already a goal down to Gary Speed's free-kick.

And, within two minutes of his arrival, Liverpool were two down, courtesy of an Ivan Campo header, and on their way to another disappointing Premiership defeat.

The game was not without controversy, though, and Benitez was unhappy with the referee's assistant's award of the 30th minute free-kick from which Speed gave the home side the lead. The linesman flagged for handball against Reina as the goalkeeper was in the process of kicking the ball from his hands, and the Anfield boss was furious with the decision.

He moaned, 'It's clear that a mistake has been made. Pepe let go of the ball inside the area and then kicked it outside. The linesman was in a bad position. I knew at the time it was a mistake, but what can you do? Every week we can talk about incidents, but nothing changes. It's annoying.'

It was another damaging defeat in Liverpool's pursuit of the title, and it left them six points behind leaders Manchester United and Chelsea. Benitez, however, remained upbeat.

He insisted, 'We know what was said when we lost two in a row earlier in the season and then we won two games quickly to change things. Now it is important to be calm and believe it is too soon to make judgements about the title. We can talk now about the problem, but two wins in a row will put us back in a challenging position.

'This is a bad time with an international break now, but afterwards we must keep winning our home games and start to do the same away. People will ask me now about the title and our chances. Maybe if we win two games in a row then the question will be different in a couple of weeks.

'I am used to such questions, but for us we must wait and see if we can get three points next time. I do not accept that rotation and changing the team is the problem. I have been told that Manchester United won the title once and Sir Alex Ferguson changed the side 38 times.'

It's debatable whether or not the international break came at a good time for Liverpool, but for Crouch it represented a chance to get two games under his belt and to rediscover his match sharpness.

With Rooney back from suspension for the Euro 2008 qualifiers against Macedonia and Croatia, he was certain to go back into the side, leaving the one remaining place to be contested between Crouch, Defoe and the recalled Andy Johnson.

Johnson had been in superb form at the start of the season following his summer move from Crystal Palace to Everton, and McClaren admitted that he was making a strong case for inclusion in the side. But when he was forced to withdraw from the squad it meant a call-up from the Under-21 squad for Charlton's Darren Bent, and the guarantee that Crouch would start alongside Rooney.

Whether McClaren would have started with Johnson in place of Crouch we will never know, but the England head coach certainly had no doubts about the Liverpool striker, who was on the hottest of hot streaks at international level.

He said in his media briefing, 'His goal-scoring record is unbelievable. You can't knock it and, once again, he answered [the critics] in the week when he scored for Liverpool in the Champions League.

'They're not just goals, they're terrific goals as well. And I've seen him do that in training, too. He's not just 6ft 7in standing there – he's got great touch, great feet, great awareness. He's improving all the time and he's scoring goals.'

For his part, Crouch was delighted to see Rooney back in the international fold and admitted that he couldn't wait to link up again with the Manchester United star, who had been strangely out of form for his club in the early stages of the season.

Crouch told reporters, 'It always gives the lads a lift when Wayne is back and it is great to have him in the squad. He is always bubbly around the place. At times, things don't go for you at club level, but he has looked lively in training and I hope it will come good for him again.

'Wayne is a top talent. People are making a big thing about his form, but you have to remember he is only young and that he is a top player. Obviously I have trained alongside him and I think my partnership with Wayne can be a success for England.'

By now, Crouch was used to receiving a warm welcome from England fans and he was no longer the target of the boo-boys. And he believed he had done enough to win over his detractors.

He said, 'Personally I feel I have done enough, but other people might take a different view. I will keep trying to improve and do more, but as long as I'm pleasing my manager and team-mates that's all I can do.

'I'm playing Champions League football with Liverpool, we're challenging for things at club level and I'm playing international football. I'm doing OK on those stages and hopefully I can keep that going.

'Everyone I meet on the streets is complimentary to me, so I seem to be turning a few people around. I don't know if it has changed since the World Cup. When you are playing for a high-profile club like Liverpool, people see a lot more of you and see I can play.

'It's the same at international level. Now people are seeing me play a lot more, whereas in the past they'd make a judgement without having seen me.'

Crouch was also keen to add to his impressive goals tally of 11 in 14 matches in an England shirt. He added, 'I want to continue my goal-scoring record. We have got two important games coming up. Macedonia surprised us in the first game, but I hope it will be a different game this weekend and we know the pitch will be a lot better at Old Trafford. Hopefully we can beat them by a bigger margin.'

But for all the confident talk in the build-up of claiming a morale-boosting victory ahead of the tough-looking trip to Croatia the following midweek, England failed to perform on the pitch in a miserable display.

The closest they came to breaking the deadlock was Gerrard's strike six minutes from time that crashed back off the bar, but Macedonia held out for a deserved 0–0 draw as McClaren suffered his first setback as England boss after three straight wins in his first three matches.

The England head coach admitted afterwards, 'It's a reality check for everybody. We have to work harder and make sure we are better in the next game. We were not good enough going forward, our passing, our final ball and our final finish. It wasn't clinical. If you look at the game overall a draw was probably a fair result, but we are very disappointed.

'We know that was not good enough. We were playing Macedonia at home and we expect to score in our home games. We did well to keep a clean sheet and get the point, but we have to do better.

'I am disappointed and frustrated, and so are the players in the changing room. Looking at the performance it has got to be better.'

Crouch was twice denied by Macedonian goalkeeper Jane Nikoloski, but, with the service from the flanks patchy at best, he was forced to admit that he had endured a frustrating afternoon. But he insisted that his partnership with Rooney could flourish.

He said, 'I enjoyed played alongside Wayne and there is still more to come from us. I don't know if Wayne is frustrated, but we are just pleased to have him back and come the next game he will be firing again.

'I was always going to have a day when my scoring run finished and when you don't score it is very disappointing, but hopefully against Croatia that run will start again for both me and Wayne. This is the first setback, but it is all about how we respond to this.

'We have kept a clean sheet and we will go into the Croatia game taking confidence from the first three games we have played under Steve McClaren. But take nothing away from Macedonia, they came here and played really well and they are a good team. We had chances, the goalkeeper made some saves and we hit the woodwork, it was just one of those days.'

It was a major setback to drop two home points against Macedonia, and there was further bad news when Gerrard's yellow card – his second of the qualifying campaign so far – ruled him out of the trip to Zagreb just four days later.

Croatia had not lost a competitive match at home for 12 years, a run that stretched to 29 games, so no one was under any illusions as to the task ahead.

'Potentially Croatia away is our hardest fixture in the group,' admitted midfielder Frank Lampard. 'We've got to go there and stand up to a good technical team and a hostile crowd, and show what we are as a team.

'Croatia are tactically a good team as well. I watched them in the World Cup against Brazil and they gave them a really tough game. That's the kind of players they have got. They always produce players from a young age, technically good players who have a bit of an edge to them. They are determined and will be desperate to beat us.

'It is important to stay together as a team. We are a realistic bunch and know that, when you are winning games and think you have the hang of it, things can go wrong. We have to look at the negatives and the things we didn't do right against Macedonia and make them right. But we have to stay positive.'

Assistant coach Terry Venables also highlighted the need for the players to relish the task facing them in Zagreb. He told thefa.com, 'We've got to make sure that we are going there looking forward to taking up the challenge. It is a very big game and a big challenge. We know they have not lost a home qualifier and that record speaks for itself.

'It will be interesting for us to see where we stand after Wednesday's game. That will be our fourth game in the group and our last qualifier of the year. After that, we'll really be able to assess where we are and how we are doing.

'I think we have already picked up some of the areas where we can improve and we must learn all the time. But we must learn quickly. We have had a setback and now there is only one way to look and that is forward. We've got to take up the challenge and look forward to it.'

With several key players missing through suspension and injury, including three of the World Cup midfield in Gerrard, Hargreaves and Joe Cole, it was widely reported that McClaren would switch to a 3-5-2 formation.

He admitted on the eve of the match, 'We've got to change and look at different systems. You have to look at the make-up of the team and we're missing a lot of players and we have to cope with that. You have to be flexible.

'We've done the work and I'm pleased with the reaction of the players so far. You can't gamble – you have to know. And I'm quite confident after seeing them that they can do it. If we have to go to three at the back, many of the players have done it before and it's no problem.'

And McClaren remained in bullish mood, despite the previous Saturday's disappointing display against Macedonia. He added, 'We need character, we need pride, we need passion and attitude. We need a team of men out there who have the experience to handle the occasion. The make-up of the team will be around those ingredients.

'Croatia are a patriotic nation, very proud. But so are we – absolutely. John Terry epitomises that. And we'll be looking for a big reaction. Everybody has to seize responsibility, we can't carry anybody. We'll be looking at the leaders in the side to help us come out on top.'

Once again, though, England talked a good game but played a poor one. McClaren did indeed switch to a 3-5-2 formation, but, with Gary Neville and Ashley Cole being deployed as wing-backs, England lacked the width to get forward, particularly on the right-hand side, where Neville's natural defensive instincts predictably hampered him.

The tactical confusion meant England often found themselves with five at the back and with the midfield being over-run. That obviously led to a lack of supply to the front two and resulted in another night of frustration for Crouch and Rooney.

Croatia won the game with a looping header from their naturalised Brazilian Eduardo Da Silva and a comedy own goal from Neville. The Manchester United star rolled a backpass towards Paul Robinson to clear but, just as the Tottenham goalkeeper went to strike the ball, it bounced up off a divot on the edge of the six-yard box and over his foot, before rolling agonisingly into the net.

That slapstick moment just about summed up England's woeful performance and for McClaren the honeymoon period was truly over. But the head coach remained confident that England would still qualify for the finals in Austria and Switzerland.

He said, 'There are a lot of games left to play and, although we've had two disappointing games, we'll move on. There are lot of points still to play for and we'll be OK. We have to stick together and turn it around.

'We have learned from all the experiences in the last four games and we will make sure we are going in the right direction. I think we can become a side which achieves things.'

The bad news for McClaren and England was that, following the defeat in Croatia, it would be five months before the side's next qualifier against Israel. That is a long time to have to reflect on a bad performance.

McClaren's players, of course, did not have so long to dwell on their shortcomings in Zagreb as they were all back in Premiership action for their clubs the following weekend.

For Crouch, that meant a home game against Blackburn as he looked to put the disappointment of his England scoring run coming to an end behind him. And, with Kuyt having picked up an injury on international duty with Holland, it was Crouch and Bellamy who lined up at Anfield to face the latter's former club.

Typically, as so often happens in football, Bellamy had the 'Ex-Factor' against his old club, scoring his first Premiership goal for Liverpool against them to earn his side a point. But, ultimately, it represented another unsatisfactory afternoon for the Reds.

Benitez admitted, 'We must be disappointed because we haven't won the game. I felt it was there to be won in the second half and we created enough chances to take all three points.

'We conceded a bad goal in the first half and we made a mistake when our two centre-halves were in a bad position, but I was pleased with the way we responded in the second half.

'We knew it would be a difficult game because Blackburn are a tough team to play against, but the reaction of the players in the second half was really good.'

That battling draw set Liverpool up for their third Champions League group clash of the season, and a potentially awkward trip to Bordeaux. The French side were certain to be up for the challenge having picked up just one point from their first two matches, and Benitez felt that could work in Liverpool's favour.

A defeat would almost certainly end Bordeaux's European challenge and the Liverpool boss said, 'They know they need to win and, if they don't, it could be the end for them. They need to go forward and attack and we must be solid in defence. 'We must not make mistakes like we did against Galatasaray. If you win in the Champions League in these big games, it can give the team more confidence for the games to come.'

And win they did, courtesy of Crouch's 56th-minute header from Bellamy's corner. It was Liverpool's 150th European victory and kept them on top of the group on goal difference ahead of PSV Eindhoven, who won 2–1 in Galatasaray.

And Benitez was delighted with his team. He said, 'It's

a good win for the confidence and a big boost for the players. The lads worked really hard, scored a good goal and could have scored others.

'We also kept a clean sheet which was good for us. It was a pity we didn't add a second goal, because that would have made the difference between a comfortable end and a nervous end to the game where we had some problems. The way the group is working out, this was a very important game to win.'

And the Spaniard was also happy with Crouch, adding, 'I was pleased with Peter Crouch. He missed a couple in the first half, but what you must do is to keep going for them, and that is what he did. For a striker the key is to keep going, you must have that mentality if you want to win anything. And that is what Peter did.'

The solitary strike against Bordeaux was Crouch's third goal in two European games following his brace against Galatasaray, and the striker was convinced Liverpool could go all the way in the competition and repeat their heroics in Istanbul in May 2005.

After the game, he insisted, 'Of course we believe we can go all the way again. I think we have more strength in depth than when we won it last time, and with a little bit of luck I'm sure we can be serious contenders.'

That victory in France was Liverpool's first of the season on the road and, as they approached their next match – a crucial Premiership trip away to bitter rivals Manchester United – Benitez was hoping that their success in the Champions League could kick-start their domestic challenge.

He said, 'I think that game can help a lot for sure.

When you play away in the Champions League and you win and keep another clean sheet, I think that's important for the confidence.

'Maybe it would have been different for us if we'd won at Sheffield United on the first day of the season. We would have had more confidence. We can't change that now, though, and we must deal with the situation we are in and be mentally strong.

'The players know how important Sunday is and the rivalry between the teams. It can be a starting point for us to change things, particularly away from home.

'It is a good opportunity for us to change things. It is a long race, and, while we know it is difficult to beat the top teams, we know we have to play them at home in the second half of the season. We need to keep going. It's important people realise we have more chances to come.

'And it is important to keep the confidence in the players. When you have confidence, you play better. And when you play better, you score more goals and win more games.'

For many Liverpool fans, matches against United are the most important games of the season, and victory means a huge amount to them. But, while Benitez recognises that, he was also keen to stress that every game is vital.

He added, 'I think it's really important, but not the most important. You never know which is going to be the most important. Maybe at the end of the season we will talk about games which were more important than this one because we were playing for the top of the table.'

His players, however, were in no doubt as to how vital the game was, with goalkeeper Reina stressing that defeat would signal an end to their dreams of a first league title for 16 years.

He told the club's website, 'We know we are losing ground. We are too far behind, eight points behind Manchester United. That's too many points. We have to keep going and fighting for everything, but if they win it will be 11 points between us, and that could be too much.

'We have to try and win there, although we know it won't be easy. We have to react in the right way and win that very important game. You never know, but 11 points at this early point of the season could prove too much to make up. We have to go there and at least try to win that match.'

Meanwhile, Crouch was hoping 'home' advantage could work in his favour as he set about trying to upset United. By now, he was living in Alderley Edge, in Cheshire, a place where many of the Old Trafford stars also live. His near neighbours include Wayne Rooney, Wes Brown, Rio Ferdinand, Edwin van der Sar and even United boss Sir Alex Ferguson.

And Crouch, who of course scored the winner against United in the FA Cup the previous season and who had a superb record for England at Old Trafford, knew that beating their great north-west rivals would be the perfect way to record Liverpool's first away win of the Premiership season.

He told the club's website, 'It doesn't get much tougher than this week has been for us, in Europe and now at Manchester United, but that win in Bordeaux has given us a huge lift, and at last we have shown we can win away this season.

'We have at least got our self-belief back. We know

some of our results have not been up to scratch, so we wanted to make our mark in Bordeaux, and that is what we achieved. Now we must do the same on the road in the Premier League, and Manchester United is as good a place as any to start.

'We would like to think we can go on the sort of run we managed at the end of last season. We feel we can play better and hopefully it will start at Old Trafford.'

Firstly, of course, Crouch had to get in the team and he admitted that his goal in Bordeaux was no guarantee that would be the case. After all, on the previous occasion when he found the net in Europe, with two goals, including his stunning scissors kick, against Galatasaray, he had found himself dropped to the bench for the next game against Bolton.

And, when Benitez named his team for the Sunday-lunchtime clash, Crouch found that history had repeated itself and that he was named yet again among the substitutes. And this despite the fact that Bellamy was missing through injury.

Instead, Benitez opted to play Kuyt as a lone striker in front of a five-man midfield as he altered his team for the 96th game in succession. Sadly for him and Liverpool, his tactics backfired badly.

They were second best throughout the game and slumped to a dismal 2–0 defeat, with United clinching the three points thanks to strikes from Paul Scholes and Rio Ferdinand. It was a disastrous result for the Reds and left them 11 points behind the leading pair of Manchester United and Chelsea, and with little or no hope of clawing back that deficit in the months ahead.

Benitez, however, refused to write off his side's title chances completely. He said, 'It's clear it was a very disappointing day for us. I think we started the game well and created a couple of chances, but if you score first it can change things and we are not doing that at the moment.

'The players worked really hard, but when they scored the second goal it then became difficult for us to create chances. They are a very good team with a lot of quality. I know we are 11 points behind, but you can change things by working harder and doing the things we were doing well last season.

'There is still a long way to go in the season. How do you change things in your life? By working better and harder. That is what we will do.

'Now is the time for the manager, the captain and all my staff to work together to help all the players. I said to the players straight after the game that there's nothing they can do about what happened now, but they have to show everyone they have character. We know they have the quality, but maybe sometimes you need even more than this.

'When you're Liverpool Football Club, you know you have a responsibility to try to win every game and play well. Maybe this is not always possible, but it's what we try to do. In the first 25 minutes [against Manchester United], we were OK. We had possession in attacking areas, but didn't create clear chances.

'The players worked hard, but it's clear we need to rebuild their confidence now. We can only do this by training and winning games. It's not going to happen in two games, but over a longer period.

'Key players are not at their level. We have a strong spine to our team, but if you analyse things you can see where we need to improve.'

And there were words of comfort for Benitez and his players when Old Trafford chief Ferguson insisted nothing had been decided by the outcome of one match. In his post-match press conference, he claimed, 'I would not dismiss Liverpool. They have a good run-in and there will be a freshness about them in the second half of the season because of the way Rafa has been ringing the changes.

'Results in these matches cannot have a decisive influence; it is far too early for that. People were dismissing Arsenal a few weeks ago, now it is Liverpool. It is just crazy.'

But, while Benitez and Ferguson were insisting Liverpool still had a role to play in the title race, former Anfield heroes were queuing up to pour scorn on that suggestion. And the finger of blame was being pointed in the direction of the manager for his constant chopping and changing of his playing personnel.

Mark Lawrenson wrote in his column in the *Liverpool Post*, 'Eleven points behind the leaders, Liverpool can forget about winning the title. Instead, Rafael Benitez should now concentrate on getting back to basics to rescue his team's season.

'It was such a disappointing performance at Manchester United. The players appeared devoid of ideas and a little bit characterless, which is alarming given the importance of the game. Ask Liverpool supporters what they wanted from this season, the answer would be to win the league. So what's gone wrong?

'I don't particularly think United were that much better, but they certainly had more about them and actually looked like they knew what they were doing. That's the problem for Liverpool at the moment. With all the changes Benitez makes to the starting line-up and the influx of new arrivals, it's been impossible for the players to build up an understanding of each other's game.

'Players like the ability to know what their colleagues are going to do when things start going against them. There's nothing better. But Benitez's rotation policy is making that impossible. If only to build some confidence and cohesion, Benitez should play his best team and stick to it for a while. Forget about different systems and formations. Keep the spine of the team the same, the shape the same, the defence the same.

'If you pick your best team virtually every single week and it then doesn't work over a period of time, then you know it's not going to work. Right now, Liverpool don't know what will and won't work.

'But does Benitez know what his best team is? With all this chopping and changing, I doubt it.'

Ronnie Whelan, a former team-mate of Lawrenson at Anfield, was equally scathing in his assessment of Benitez's selection policy, particularly his treatment of Crouch and his fellow strikers.

He told the *Sun*, 'If you go back in history, you will find most successful clubs have had two centre-forwards with a great understanding who would score goals and feed off each other week in and week out.

'At Liverpool, you just have to think of Ian Rush and Kenny Dalglish, and Kevin Keegan and John Toshack.

Now it's Bellamy and Crouch in one game, Kuyt and Crouch in the next, then Kuyt and Luis Garcia or any number of other permutations.

'You cannot get an understanding going. It's the same for two central defenders or two full-backs who play together regularly. They know where they will be at any given time. But with the rotation system I don't think you can get that same understanding.'

And Phil Thompson, a former Liverpool great and the man who worked as assistant manager alongside Gerard Houllier at Anfield, added on Sky Sports News, 'I've been a party to rotation, so it's difficult for me to sit here and say he shouldn't rotate, but when you have four, five or six changes each week it is difficult for the players to get an understanding.

'I don't think he knows his best team, I really don't. With the players he's brought in – and he's brought a lot of good quality – the problem is, what is his best XI? Even he doesn't know!

'If you look at the team, he keeps chopping and changing and even when everybody is fit. I don't think he could say, or write down on the blackboard in his office, what his best team is.'

And for Crouch, the frustration at being in and out of the team was beginning to take its toll. At the start of the season, when he was given a regular run of games, he scored eight goals in his first seven games for club and country.

Since scoring for England against Macedonia though, the sixth successive game in which he'd scored, having started all six of them, his run was just three goals in ten games for Liverpool and England.

He'd scored all three of those goals for his club, in eight games, but significantly the goals came in the four games in which he'd started. In the four in which he had appeared as a substitute, he had drawn a blank.

There was no doubt that the rotation policy was seriously damaging his form. On the eve of the United match, he had admitted in an interview with Sky Sports, 'It is frustrating at times when you've played well and then you find yourself on the bench for the next game.

'I can understand in a way the manager's thinking because we've got a lot of games in all the competitions we're involved in, and he's got a big squad, and a good squad, so he can chop and change.

'But as a player you want to be selfish and you want to be playing every game.'

And when you score in virtually every game you start, as Crouch had done, you can feel entitled to expect to be picked every week, can't you?

Clearly not if you play for a team managed by Señor Benitez.